THE TRAGEDY OF PROGRESS

THE TRAGEDY OF PROGRESS

MARXISM, MODERNITY AND THE ABORIGINAL QUESTION

David Bedford
Danielle Irving

FERNWOOD PUBLISHING • HALIFAX

Dedication

To Riiko Olivia Bedford

Editing: Donna Davis
Design and production: Beverley Rach
Printed and bound in Canada by: Hignell Printing Limited

A publication of:
Fernwood Publishing
Box 9409, Station A
Halifax, Nova Scotia
B3K 5S3

Fernwood Publishing Company Limited gratefully acknowledges the financial support of the Department of Canadian Heritage and the Canada Council for the Arts for our publishing program.

Le Conseil des Arts du Canada | The Canada Council for the Arts

Canadian Cataloguing in Publication Data

Bedford, David, 1954-
The tragedy of progress: Marxism, modernity and the Aboriginal question

(Basics from Fernwood Publishing)
Includes bibliographical references.
ISBN 1-55266-050-8

1. Native peoples—Canada—Social conditions. 2. Communism—Canada.
3. Socialism—Canada. I. Irving, Danielle. II. Title. III. Series.

E78.C2B4182 2001 335.4'089'97071 C00-901780-1

CONTENTS

Part Two

ACKNOWLEDGEMENTS

Although we often believe that our ideas are our own, they rarely are. We would like to thank at least some of those friends from whom our ideas ultimately sprang. In particular, we acknowledge the great debt owed to Andrea Bear Nicholas, Chair of Native Studies at St. Thomas University and foremost historian of the Maliseet peoples; and Sidney Pobihushchy, retired Chair of Political Science at the University of New Brunswick. Thom Workman, a colleague and frequent collaborator, read the manuscript with great care and made many valuable suggestions. Debbie Sloan provided technical support and assistance in all phases of the writing, without which the manuscript would not have been completed. Finally, we must thank our spouses Sue Tatemichi and Brian Stephens for reasons too numerous to begin listing.

INTRODUCTION

ABORIGINAL CRISIS AND THE SILENCE OF THE LEFT

The 1990s have been dominated, unlike any previous decade, by issues relating to the relationship between Aboriginal communities and the Canadian state. 1990 witnessed the Oka crisis in which groups of Mohawk warriors took up armed resistance against the municipal government of Oka, Quebec. City leaders planned to extend a golf course by cutting down a pine forest sacred to the Mohawk people. Resistance soon spread to Kahnawake, a large Mohawk reserve on the south shore of Montreal. Years of expropriation of the reserve lands for the building of roads and bridges to serve Montreal had left Kahnawake in a strategic position. Mohawk warriors seized this advantage and, for two months, blockaded the Mercier Bridge and adjacent roads, bringing traffic on the south shore to a standstill. Despite support for the Mohawk cause from a number of quarters—spontaneous donations of food from a number of Montreal's ethnic communities, for example—others expressed frightening hostility. Spurred on by popular local radio personality, Gilles Proulx, an angry mob gathered at the Montreal end of the Mercier bridge and stoned a caravan of cars transporting the very young and the elderly away from the reserve to safety. One elderly man was seriously injured when a rock crashed through his car window and hit him. The residents of Kahnawake also witnessed nightly orgies of hate as citizens of neighbouring Chateauguay hung and burned effigies in rituals clearly reminiscent of Klan violence.

Government officials and opinion leaders must take the lion's share of the blame for the tensions and hostile atmosphere. Their inflamed rhetoric and provocative actions encouraged the excesses that marked the summer of 1990. Food supplies were cut off; supporters of the Mohawks, or indeed anyone who looked "Indian," were harassed, while thousands of soldiers with tanks, helicopters and machine guns added to the atmosphere of fear and crisis. However, perhaps most troubling of all for those sympathetic to the Mohawk struggle for justice was the absence of support from the working class in both Quebec and the rest of Canada. A show of support from organized labour could have helped end the crisis in its early days, yet none was forthcoming. Clearly, labour did not see its interests tied to the success of the Mohawk struggle.

As the 1990s came to a close, the news was again dominated by an "Aboriginal issue." This time the spark did not come from a small group of Aboriginal militants defending their lands. Rather, the situation was set ablaze by a decision taken by the Supreme Court of Canada in September 1999. The case involved, ironically, an individual, Donald Marshall, who had previously achieved notoriety for having been unjustly imprisoned for eleven years for a murder he did not commit. In 1993, his "crime" was to catch and sell 210 kilograms of eels out of season. For countless generations Mi'kmaw people have lived by harvesting fish, lobster, clams and other seafood. A treaty signed with the British in 1760, one of a series of eighteenth-century treaties, recognized the new right of British settlement as well as the traditional right of the Mi'kmaw to live by fishing, hunting, cutting and so on. These rights have been claimed and verified by the Supreme Court from time to time, but the governments of Nova Scotia and New Brunswick have regularly refused to recognize the Supreme Court decisions (Bear Nicholas 1994: 4–6). The Supreme Court decided in the Marshall case that those covered by the treaty had the right to earn a "moderate living by fishing."

The events that followed were dispiriting. Despite the small number of Aboriginal fishers some non-Native fishers reacted angrily to the decision. The main trouble-spot is the lobster fishery. Non-Native lobster fishers in the Maritimes need a federal license to catch lobster. They also have limits placed on the number of traps they can set, the size of lobster they can keep and the seasons during which they can fish. Aboriginal fishers, while also bound by size restrictions and an overall need for conservation, are allowed to set traps and sell their catch at any time. They may make only "a moderate living" from the fishery, however, which means that no one Aboriginal fisher can catch and sell more than would provide food, clothing, shelter and other necessities for his or her family. Some non-Native fishers reacted violently despite the fact that of the total of roughly two million lobster traps set in the Maritimes only twelve thousand, or about 0.6 percent of the total, were set by Native fishers.

The days following the initial decision were marked by violence. Non-Native fishers were upset at what they felt were "special" rights for

Aboriginal fishers, and they expressed their opposition as a concern for conservation. The worst confrontations took place near the Burnt Church reserve in New Brunswick. There, over one hundred non-Native fishing boats were used to destroy the traps of Native fishers. A Native ceremonial structure was burned, and a Mi'kmaw man injured when the truck he was driving was rammed. Threats and intimidation occurred throughout fishing communities in the Maritimes. The violence stemmed in part from ignorance, as some non-Native fishers exaggerated the threat to the lobster stocks and their livelihoods. It also stemmed from government inaction and media overreaction. The government never took the lead in quelling fears, and the media continually referred to the situation in inflated terms, describing it as a "battle" or a "war," and by raising the spectre that many natural resource industries would fall under significant Native control.

As in the Oka crisis, organized labour failed to take significant initiatives to ease tensions and forge alliances. Few, if any, of the voices heard portrayed Aboriginal fishers, or loggers or hunters, as anything other than a threat to the interests of non-Natives. As through much of their history, Aboriginal peoples have found themselves struggling nearly alone.

The non-Native community is confused by the court rulings of the 1990s that have recognized a few of the long-standing and long-ignored treaty rights. The Paul case in 1998 gave Aboriginal persons in New Brunswick right of access to timber on Crown land, although that decision was overturned in the Provincial Superior Court. Other decisions have extended hunting and fishing rights in various regions of Canada. Many Canadians, led by the Canadian Alliance (then Reform) Party, have called for the abolition of Indian status and the treatment of every Canadian as "equal." This means that in future there would be no status Indians, no reserves and, importantly, no treaties or treaty rights. Like the 1969 White Paper initiative of Trudeau's then Minister of Indian Affairs, Jean Chrétien, the recent demands of the Canadian Alliance would solve the "Aboriginal question" by denying the existence of anything Aboriginal in Canada. Surely, they argue, enough time has passed since European civilization became dominant, surely the process of assimilation is far enough advanced, surely the culture of the Western world is attractive enough that we can tear up the treaties and finally relegate "Aboriginalness" to the history books for good. When the federal government announces that settling all outstanding treaty, land and other claims could cost taxpayers as much as $200 billion, one can see why the Canadian Alliance position is attractive for some (Scofield 1999b: A3).

This past decade was also marked by a four-year, $60-million-dollar Royal Commission; the stand-off at Gustafsen Lake; and the tragic killing of Dudley George. Most significant of all, perhaps, is the Nisga'a Agreement, which resolves a centuries-old land claim by the Nisga'a of Northwest British Columbia. As reported in the *Globe and Mail:*

> The agreement grants the Nisga'a people the right to self-government over about 2,000 square kilometres in northwestern British Columbia and $487.1 million in benefits and cash. The Nisga'a people will begin paying taxes and they have given up their rights to further claims. (Scofield 1999a: A4)

The agreement, which is awaiting final Parliamentary approval, has created much controversy. While the details of the agreement have been questioned, the principal criticism has come from those who argue that it creates a racially based government. Such criticisms stand on the modern, liberal notion that each person *qua* citizen must be equal under the law. Canada, it is argued, should be a nation of equal citizens with no special rights or privileges for a province, a group or a person.

In a society so infused with liberal ideas as ours, this rhetoric has a powerful appeal to all classes. Ironically, its appeal is even greater for those who experience oppression of various kinds in their lives. If I have to work hard, make do and so on, so the rhetoric goes, why should someone else get special status, be it linguistic or cultural privilege or a right to access resources? It is not uncommon to hear opposition to particular rights for Quebec combined with similar criticisms of what are perceived the unique privileges of status Indians. The oppressed often interpret inequities in society as the result of the special treatment accorded others. This can easily translate into opposition to anything that resembles difference. As citizens of the same state special rights cannot be justified on liberal ideological grounds. How then can supporters of the Nisga'a or the Mi'kmaw fishers justify a right unique to these groups? Within the liberal paradigm there is really no answer to such a question.

We respond to these questions in two ways: the first takes account of the history of the relationship between Aboriginal communities and the Canadian state and the second draws on the uniqueness of their traditional cultures. First, it is misleading at best to argue against the exercise of treaty rights by saying that all should be equal citizens. Contracts, licenses and other legal documents recognize that different citizens can do different things. This is commonplace. In addition, the *Indian Act* already places status Indians living on-reserve in a legally unique, and decidedly inferior, position and has done so unabated since 1876. Second, and of greater interest to us, Aboriginal cultures are not simply one more strand of a multicultural tapestry. Their traditions, which probably most Aboriginal persons want to preserve, are not easily compatible with the bourgeois, liberal democracy to which the remainder of Canada is committed. Being treated as equal Canadians amounts to cultural genocide. Of course, this is not to imply that traditional forms of governance did not value equality or freedom. Rather, we must be mindful that treating the founding ideals of modern Western culture as ubiquitous forces behaviours, forms of interaction, economic values and political values onto peoples whose traditions are incommensurate with our own. A consequence of such forced imposition has been the crises in Aboriginal–state relations and within Aboriginal communities themselves, which we are presently witnessing.

The system in which tiny reserves are governed by a band council sanctioned by the Department of Indian and Northern Affairs does not appear to be working. Reserves suffer from chronic housing shortages. The people living there endure much greater poverty, live substantially shorter lives and suffer much higher unemployment than most others living in Canada. Most cruelly, they see their children commit suicide in epidemic proportions. Substance abuse is high because feelings of hopelessness are omnipresent. Leaving the reserve offers little hope. The mainstream culture of Canada's urban areas is often a hostile place, as racism only compounds these other problems.

Many Canadians are confused by Native–non-Native confrontations, legal and political challenges to the status quo and the continued existence of a marginalized population. The limbo of the reserve system was never intended as a long-term arrangement. Reserves were the stepping stone to assimilation, holding pens where the Aboriginalness of the first people could be more easily washed away, even if, in an irony of history, their very isolation helped protect Aboriginal culture. The choice presently facing Aboriginal peoples is between the two equally difficult options of modernity and tradition. Choosing to embrace modernity requires no analysis, no strategy, no allies. While such a decision may be difficult in practice, it is easy to think out theoretically. One need only adopt the way of life of the majority: work in a factory or office; consume; live as a free, liberal citizen in the universal, homogeneous state. Choosing traditional life is more difficult. What resources are needed to reinvigorate these traditions? How can they be acquired? How can the pervasiveness of the ideology of modernity be counteracted?

The search for answers to these questions and the struggle to implement them is going on daily. Efforts are being made to recover and use Native languages that have largely fallen into disuse. A Mohawk immersion school in Kahnawake serves as a model for many communities, encouraging them to set up schools on-reserve to teach the young traditional values. Ceremonies are being practised with greater frequency. Important as these steps are, though, they do not address the most fundamental issue, which is that a culture, a way of life, involves at its base an economy, a set of practices and ideas concerning how a community makes its living. Traditional cultures were based on economic practices vastly different from our own. Dominique Temple (1988) describes it as the difference between a reciprocal economy in which sharing is the fundamental value, and an exchange economy in which competition and taking advantage are the core ideals. Traditional Aboriginal economies, particularly in the northeastern part of Turtle Island (or North America), were based on the land and the free, unrestricted access of everyone to its resources. The land was honoured as the source of life. There was little private accumulation (the most respected persons were those who gave away the most), and there was no hierarchy of persons. Not only could land not be sold, almost nothing could be sold. We, on the other hand, will buy and sell almost everything, from human organs to ideas and to genetic codes. The majority in modern, liberal–bourgeois societies who lack direct access to resources must sell their labour or starve. Honours are bestowed on those whose personal hoard could feed millions upon millions in any given year.

How can the choice to live traditionally be made viable? The short answer is that physical and institutional space is needed within which a traditional economy can be practised free from encroachment by modern capitalist pressures. Achieving this will require allies. Government is not interested in helping; the past 133 years has shown us this. Even today, government contests every treaty claim, every land claim, every assertion of rights. The *Indian Act*, which is the legislative centrepiece of the relationship between the Canadian state and the Aboriginal people, has served as a model for the apartheid regime in South Africa. Business, as well, opposes any extension of a genuinely Aboriginal culture for a familiar reason. When land and resources and people exist traditionally they are no longer available for exploitation and profit. Land being used for a subsistence livelihood, whether here or elsewhere throughout the world, is off the market. No money is to be made when a peasant village consumes what it produces. "Entrepreneurial" activity is possible only when goods and labour exchange hands. There is no exchange, and hence no opportunity for entrepreneurialism, when the products of labour are consumed directly. Capitalism spread internationally through development, a process which has helped undermine self-sufficient indigenous economies, replacing them with economies based on commodity production and exchange. There is little hope that business will aid the process of preserving and protecting a traditional economy.

This leaves labour. To date, labour at best has been cool in its response to Aboriginal attempts to resist the incorporation of land and people into the modern economy. They see their jobs as dependent upon continuing exploitation of natural resources, and Aboriginal peoples seem to be standing in the way. Such a hostile stance, though, is not necessary, even if it is understandable. The working class has never lost sight of the fact that the owners of capital use their labour for profit. When wages are driven down and jobs are "lost," only to be "found" again in low-wage sectors in the developing world, labour is under no illusions about its friends and its enemies. Understanding of the source of the problem, however, often betrays the effects of ideological hegemony. For example, labour often conceives of social and economic problems in the terms of the dominant discourse. Labour, as well as business, speaks of the need to pay down the debt and put Canada's financial house in order. In addition, it has adopted much of the mythical imagery that infuses contemporary discourse: taxes are too high; everyone can make it; business must be able to make a profit; hard work is a moral value; and so on. So, despite the reading of economic developments by the working class in ways that draw attention to its opposition to the capitalist class, the working class is often caught up in the liberal worldview of the bourgeois order. The outlook and understandings of bourgeois society are so prevalent—Antonio Gramsci referred to them as "hegemonic"—that the working class often loses a clear sense of its natural friends and foes. There is, however, a now more clearly/now more dimly viewed common experience of oppression and struggle between labour and Aboriginal communities.

This should make them natural allies. However, the precise nature of their opposition to the dominant, capitalist class differs. Despite important debates within Aboriginal communities over the value of specific strategies such as self-government (Monture-Angus 1999: Chapter 1), there is widespread agreement on the need to create economic and political "space" within which traditional practices can flourish. Labour, on the other hand, wants a return to the 1950s and 1960s when secure, full-time, unionized jobs were much more common. On the surface these two agendas do not easily coalesce into a common front. Our question, then, is does the left's analysis of the Aboriginal question, and of the meaning and possibility of a traditional culture surviving in the modern world, contribute to the forging of alliances between the working-class struggle and that of Aboriginal peoples? Further, do the values that ground the left's world outlook commit it to a vision of progress in which what is Aboriginal is doomed? Is the left, and the progressive wing of the labour movement, so irreducibly modern in its presuppositions that, like the state and the interests of business, it is also hostile to a traditional way of life?

The book is divided into four chapters. Chapter 1 deals with the history of the Aboriginal peoples and their continuing struggle for survival. Chapter 2 examines the left's response to, and analysis of, this history of struggle.

Chapter 3 argues that the left's generally critical reaction to the "Aboriginal question" is based on a particular reading of Marxism. Specifically, Marxism is understood to be a variant of modernity that, like liberalism, capitalism, scientism and fetishized technology, is seen as flowing from the enlightenment idea of unceasing progress through the application of an instrumental rationality. Chapter 4 examines the reading of Marx implicit in the left's analysis of the Aboriginal question with a view to answering the question of whether or not the critique of Marxism in the Aboriginal commentators is well-founded.

PART ONE

CHAPTER 1

THE CONTINUING CONQUEST

This chapter has an ambitious goal. Aboriginal societies present no monolithic, common history, no pre-contact cultural uniformity, which seems required if one is to write such a brief survey of their pre-contact culture and post-contact history. Pre-contact Iroquoian culture differed dramatically from that of the Montagnais, and even more so from the fishery-based societies on the west coast of Turtle Island. Similarly, post-contact experiences display a range of relationships. Some societies are governed by treaties; others are not. Some societies have not formally surrendered sovereignty; others have (Frideres 1998: Chapter 3). The extent of contact and colonization also differs. What follows is selective. The justification for choosing to discuss the specific events that we do is the coherence it brings to the complexities of the present condition of Aboriginal–state relationships.

PRE-CONTACT CULTURE

Naturally, there was enormous variety among Aboriginal cultures. We will focus on the Iroquois for two reasons. First, Iroquois political, social and spiritual understandings were recorded in a document, the *Great Law of Peace*, which has been preserved. This provides a remarkable source of information on pre-contact culture. Second, the *Great Law* is still a living idea. Many, perhaps most, people in Iroquois communities continue to adhere to its principles. While the full degree to which lives are actually lived according to the teachings of the *Great Law of Peace* is an open question, it is beyond doubt that it is still, in public discourse at least, an authoritative document.

The *Great Law of Peace* was written a century or so before the first Europeans reached Turtle Island (Johansen 1982: 21–22), and it united five previously warring nations (Mohawk, Oneida, Onondaga, Cayuga and Seneca) into what became known as the Five Nations Confederacy. In the early 1700s the Tuscarora nation joined, completing the Six Nations Confederacy that still exists today. By legend, the League, as the Confederacy is sometimes called, was founded by a Huron named Deganawidah (also spelled "Tekanawita"). The five nations had been warring, and their societies were degenerating in the continuing blood feuds. From across the waters of Lake Ontario came the Peacemaker, Deganawidah, who brought a message of peace through reasoned moderation. He first converted Hiawatha, who thereafter acted as his spokesperson. Together they convinced the Mohawk nation that war and strife could be overcome if all people put down their weapons and lived guided by reason. Eventually all five nations were converted, including the fearsome Atotarho, who was the leader of the Onondaga and the most terrible of all warriors; according to legend, he ate his victims. When Atotarho saw that the message of peace through reasoned moderation had great power in uniting the people, he relented and was made Chief of the League.

The *Great Law of Peace*, however, is more than simply a document establishing a confederacy. It is to the Iroquois what the poetry of Homer is to Greek society—the political, social and spiritual articulation of their culture. It contains 117 sections or "wampum." Wampum are strings of coloured shells that form intricate patterns. Reportedly discovered by Hiawatha, they are mnemonic devices and are sacred to the Iroquois. Solemn occasions, such as treaty signings, are recorded in wampum. The wampum of the *Great Law* cover a wide range of topics, from details regarding decision-making in the Confederacy to clan structures and relations and even burial rituals.

The most pressing need for the establishment of the League was to bring peace. Wampum 65 spells this out:

> I, Tekanawita [Deganawidah], and the United Chiefs, now uproot the tallest tree (*skarenhesekowa*) and into the hole thereby made we cast all weapons of war. Into the depths of the earth, down into the deep underneath currents of water (*Tionawatetsien*) flowing to unknown regions we cast all the weapons of strife. We bury them from sight and we plant again the tree. Thus shall the Great Peace be established and hostilities shall no longer be known between the Five Nations, but peace to the United People.

Although the *Great Peace* originally included the five Iroquoian nations, Deganawidah intended his message to be a signal to other Aboriginal individuals and nations. Wampum 2 reads:

> Roots have spread out from the Tree of Great Peace, one to the north, one to the east, one to the south, and one to the west. These are the Great White Roots, and their nature is Peace and Strength.
>
> If any man or any nation outside the Five Nations shall obey the laws of the Great Peace (*Kaianerekowa*), and shall make this known to the statesmen of the League, they may trace back the roots to the Tree. If their minds are clean, and if they are obedient and promise to obey the wishes of the Council of the League, they shall be welcomed to take shelter beneath the Tree of the Long Leaves.
>
> We place at the top of the Tree of Great Peace an eagle, who is able to see afar. If he sees in the distance any danger threatening, he will at once warn the people of the League.

The League itself was a Confederacy. In fact, some have argued that it served as the model for the federal structure of the United States' Constitution (Johansen 1982). The clans of each nation were represented at the Council of the League by male chiefs, who were chosen by the elder women of the clan. Decisions were taken by consensus at all levels, from the discussions within clans to those within nations and the League. Women as well as men participated in all discussions and decisions. Chiefs were expected to carry out and transmit faithfully all decisions taken by the clans that they represented. Failure to do so invited a terrible retribution:

> A bunch of wampum strings, three spans of the hand in length, the upper half of the bunch being white and the lower half black, and formed from equal contributions of the men of the Five Nations, shall be the token that the men have combined themselves into one head, one body, and one thought, and it shall symbolize their ratification of the peace pact of the League, whereby the chiefs of the Five Nations have established the Great Peace. The white portion of the shell strings represent the women, and the black portion the men. The black portion, furthermore, is a token of power and authority vested in the men of the Five Nations.
>
> This string of wampum vests the people with the right to correct their erring Chiefs. In case a part of the chiefs or all of them pursue a course not vouched for by the people and heed not the third warning of their women relatives (Wasenensawenrate), then the matter shall be taken to the General Council of the Women of the Five Nations. If the chiefs notified and warned three times fail to heed, then the case falls into the hands of the men of the Five Nations. The War Chiefs shall then, by right of such power and

> authority, enter the open Council to warn the chief or chiefs to return from their wrong course. If the chiefs heed the warning, they shall say, "We shall reply tomorrow". If then an answer is returned in favor of justice and in accord with this Great Law, then the Chiefs shall individually pledge themselves again, by again furnishing the necessary shells for the pledge. Then the War Chief or chiefs exhort the chiefs, urging them to be just and true.
>
> Should it happen that the chiefs refuse to heed the third warning, then two courses are open: either the men may decide in their council to depose the chief or chiefs, or to club them to death with war clubs. Should they in their council decide to take the first course, the War Chief shall address the chief or chiefs, saying,
>
> *"Since you the chiefs of the Five Nations have refused to return to the procedure of the Constitution, we now declare your seats vacant, and we take off your horns, the token of your chieftainship, and others shall be chosen and installed in your seats. Therefore, vacate your seats".*
>
> Should the men in their council adopt the second course, the War Chief shall order his men to enter the council, to take positions beside the errant chiefs sitting between them wherever possible. When this is accomplished, the war chief holding in his outstretched hand a bunch of black wampum strings shall say to the erring chiefs,
>
> *"So now, chiefs of the Five Nations, harken to these last words from your men. You have not heeded the warnings of the General Council of Women, and you have not heeded the warning of the Men of the Nations, all urging you to the right course of action. Since you are determined to resist and to withhold justice from your people, there is only one course for us to adopt".*
>
> At this point, the War Chief shall drop the bunch of black wampum, and the men shall spring to their feet and club the erring chiefs to death. Any erring chief may become submissive before the War Chief lets fall the Black Wampum. Then his execution is withheld.
>
> The Black Wampum here used symbolizes that the power to execute is buried, but it may be raised up again by the men. It is buried, but when the occasion arises, they may pull it up and derive their power and authority to act as here described. (Wampum 59, original emphasis)

The forty-eight (later fifty, after the Tuscaroras joined) chiefs of the Confederacy had solely political responsibilities. Military and political power were kept separate. For example, if a Chief wished to join a war party, he first had to step down as political chief (Wampum 90). The War Chiefs also were appointed by the clan mothers; in addition to their military duties, war chiefs acted as ombudspersons, insuring that the political chiefs performed their duties properly.

Even though the Iroquois had an elaborate confederal arrangement with complex procedures for discussion and deliberation, it was not a "state society" as the term is used by social scientists. There were no methods or institutions of coercion; there were no laws to which obedience was required; there were no courts or prisons. Even war was a voluntary affair. The young men would fight, or not, at their own discretion. Therefore, great emphasis was placed on arriving at consensus. Society was held together by a clan system and by a spiritual sense of obligation and thanksgiving. The latter, for example, was codified in the requirement that, before any gathering where the people would deliberate, thanksgiving must be given to the natural world as the cradle of human being.

Thanksgiving

> Whenever the statesmen of the League shall assemble for the purpose of holding a council, the Onondaga statesmen shall open it by expressing their gratitude to their cousin statesmen, and greeting them, and they shall make an address and offer thanks to the earth where men dwell, to the streams of water, the pools and the lakes, to the maise and the fruits, to the medicinal herbs and trees, to the forest trees for their usefulness, and to the animals that serve as food and give their pelts for clothing, to the great winds and the lesser winds, to the Thunderers; to the Sun, the mighty warrior; to the moon, to the messengers of the Creator who reveals his wishes, and to the Great Creator who dwells in the heavens above who gives all the things useful to men, and who is the source and the ruler of health and life. (Wampum 7)

This invocation reiterated the groundedness of human existence in the natural order. Every decision and action had to be weighed against the obligation to preserve the basis of life for the upcoming seven generations.

The clan system further reinforced social cohesion. Lewis Henry Morgan, who first studied the League, described the clan system as its very foundation (Morgan 1962: 60). Every nation was divided into clans. The Mohawks, for example, had three clans: Bear, Wolf and Turtle. The clans were exogamous, with clan lineage being passed on through the mother (Wampum 44). Clans were also matrilocal, which meant that the husband left his family household and lived in the longhouse of his wife. The Iroquois call themselves the people of the longhouse and use the image of the longhouse to refer to the League itself. The longhouse was a wooden dwelling composed of compartments joined end to end to form a chain. Each clan in the village had a longhouse; and its separate compartments were the dwellings of nuclear families.

Property was held by the clan. "These clans distributed through their respective nations shall be the sole owners and holders of the soil of the country and in them it is vested, as a birthright" (Wampum 42). Resources were shared within the clans. If, for instance, a member of the Bear clan travelled, she or he would be welcomed by others of the Bear clan wherever they went as if part of the same family. Economic life, like political and social life, was centred around the clan as well. The Iroquois farmed extensively. The basic crops were the Three Sisters—corn, beans and squash—which were grown together. The corn was planted in rows, which acted as stakes for the beans. Squash formed a ground cover between the rows to keep down weeds. These staples were supplemented with seasonal fruits and berries and by hunting. Whatever was collected was communally prepared by the women of the clan and distributed. There was no sense that economic activity could be carried out properly by individuals.

Although this description of the important features of the culture of traditional society has focused on the Iroquois, much of it is true of other nations as well. The Maliseet and Mi'kmaw people shared much in common with the Iroquois, as did the other member nations of the Wabanaki Confederacy: the Abenaki, the Kennebec, the Penobscot and the Passamaquoddy. What all Aboriginal nations do share is a memory of traditional forms of social and economic life and of forms of governance that are significantly different from the forms brought to Turtle Island, and eventually imposed on them, by the European invaders.

Challenges to Traditional Culture

The arrival of the Europeans eventually led to the undermining of the traditional forms of life, such as those expressed in the *Great Law of Peace.* How this happened is a complex story; it varies among Aboriginal communities and has changed over time. There is, however, a general pattern to the colonial de-culturation process which has occurred and has been studied across the globe. Colonizing powers attempt to undermine the spiritual values of the local culture, transform its social and political relationships and finally, and most importantly, alter its economy. These assaults, in their detail, make up the story of the consequences of contact for Aboriginal peoples.

One example of this general pattern can be found in the writings of the anthropologist Eleanor Leacock. Leacock (1954) specialized in the effects of contact on the Montagnais, a nation that occupied the north shore of the St. Lawrence River, north and east of Quebec City. The Montagnais were an especially valuable example for study because they had preserved much of their traditional culture and their memory of it. As well, there existed extensive records of the first effects of contact in the *Jesuit Relations*, reports that recounted the experiences of the Jesuits, who were among the first Europeans whom the Montagnais met.

Leacock (1954) argued that the traditional culture of the Montagnais, which resembled the Iroquois in its relative gender equality and political and economic equality and reciprocity, was undermined by the introduction of the fur trade. After contact, long-standing economic patterns changed. French trade goods became scarce and highly prized. Those who were the source of these goods, especially the men who trapped, gradually took on increasingly important roles within the society. Although the demise of traditional culture was not immediate, and although important traces remain even today, especially in more remote areas, Leacock noted that the fundamental basis of the economy changed and other aspects of the culture followed suit. Because trapping was a male domain, the relative importance of women's roles in particular declined. As this happened, their socio-political status also fell. In a long passage, Leacock (1954: 7) summarized her argument:

> The basic dynamic of this process can perhaps best be seen by elaborating upon Herskovits' statement that it is the production for use rather than for exchange in primitive economies that focuses the attention on the products of the land rather than the land itself. Formerly the Montagnais hunted co-operatively and shared their game, which was immediately consumed by the group. They could not preserve, store, or transport food to any significant extent. Occasionally there was surplus meat to be dried and kept, but it merely filled in temporarily when hunting was poor and could not be depended upon for any length of time. Owing to the uncertainty of the hunt, several families were necessarily dependent upon each other, thus providing "a kind of subsistence insurance or greater security than individual families could achieve."
>
> With production for trade, however, the individual's most important ties, economically speaking, were transferred from within the band to without, and his objective relation to other band members changed from the co-operative to the competitive. With storable, transportable, and individually acquired supplies—principally flour and lard—as staple foods, the individual family becomes self-sufficient, and larger group living is not only superfluous in the

> struggle for existence but a positive hindrance to the personal acquisition of furs. The more furs one collects, the more material comforts one can obtain. In contrast to the Aboriginal situation, material needs become theoretically limitless.
>
> The family group begins to resent intrusions that threaten to limit its take of furs and develops a sense of proprietorship over a certain area, to which it returns year after year for the sake of greater efficiency.

Traditional Aboriginal cultures were eventually undermined by the effects of contact. Trade introduced economic relationships that had not existed previously, and these produced important changes in social and political relationships. In addition, the physical presence of Europeans caused dramatic alterations in customary patterns of life. This was especially true militarily. The arrival of Europeans meant that Aboriginal communities were brought into conflict with European nations, and communities eventually were caught up in the wars between European powers as well. The Iroquois Confederacy, for example, broke up during the American revolutionary war as the Six Nations could not agree on which side to support. The French and Indian Wars of the seventeenth century pitted Aboriginal nations against each other, as they allied themselves with either the French or the British in competition to control the fur trade.

For years the outcome of the struggle for Turtle Island was in doubt. By the mid-eighteenth century, however, diseases and the ever-increasing numbers of European invaders meant that the traditional life of Aboriginal communities was to be radically altered. What eventually emerged was the reserve system, established by the federal government through its *Indian Act* of 1876. Territories reduced by various treaties, or reserved for Aboriginal communities by practice, were legally established as reserves. Those Aboriginal persons classified as Indians fell under the jurisdiction of both the Act and those designated by the minister to administer them. The autonomy of Aboriginal communities was lost, and an alien system of politics and economics was imposed upon them.

Strategies of Assimilation

Why was the *Indian Act* and the system of segregated and isolated reserves established? Why were most Aboriginal people herded into small, isolated, highly controlled compounds? There are three interrelated answers to these questions. First, and most importantly, the European invaders wanted the resources of Turtle Island. In the early decades of colonization, this meant fur pelts. Later, as their numbers grew, the key resource was the land itself. This was most damaging to the Aboriginal peoples. While the fur trade disrupted traditional culture, the European hunger for land meant ultimate dispossession. Armed with the justifying ideology summarized by John Locke's argument that possession of the land went to those who farmed it and not to those who live with and on it, Europeans gradually took control of almost all of Turtle Island. The original inhabitants were left with as little as possible, as whatever was under Aboriginal control was not available for exploitation. Second, Europeans had no real need for the labour power of Aboriginal persons. Unlike the situation in South Africa, for example, where the development of a capitalist economy required Black labour power, in North America the numerical preponderance of Europeans meant that Aboriginal persons were not needed as part of the labour force. Therefore, they could be exterminated or quarantined without harming the economy. Finally, the federal government believed that assimilation could take place more effectively if Indians were wards of the state. By treaty, many Aboriginal communities had the right to land. By creating the political institution of the reserve, Aboriginal peoples could be placed more easily under government control. Steve Talbot (1981: 57) has summarized a similar process that took place in the United States:

> With the confinement of Indians to reservations, the conquest of the indigenous society seemed complete. What still remained, to cinch the bourgeois mission of Manifest Destiny, was the destruction of the Indian's political economy, the eradication of spiritual life and social institutions. The old collectivities were to be destroyed: tribal land and resource management, government, religion and the extended family. This was discreetly referred to as "assimilation" or "acculturation" rather than genocide.

To implement the policies of assimilation and resource accumulation the federal government passed the *Indian Act*. This comprehensive document has governed the lives of "Indians" since 1876. The first task of the Act is to define status. Who is to be covered by the Act? Section 2 defines as an "Indian" anyone "who pursuant to this Act is registered as an Indian or is entitled to be registered as an Indian." "Indian" is thus a legal classification, not a cultural or ethnic concept. Section 5 of the Act requires that "[t]here shall be maintained in the Department [of Indian Affairs] an Indian Register in which shall be recorded the name of every person who is entitled to be registered as an Indian under this Act." Each person who is legally an Indian has their name recorded as such, and they are assigned a number which identifies the band (the unit of administration) of which they are a member. According to Section 8, each band has its own list of members. While most Indians are Aboriginal, this is not always the case. Until 1985, a non-

Aboriginal woman who married an Indian man gained Indian status; Indian women who married non-Indian men lost their status as Indian.

Bands were established as the unit of administration for local affairs and for the implementation of the policies of the Minister of Indian Affairs. Each band has one or more pieces of land, "reserves," that are set aside for their use. Title, however, is held by the Crown. Individual Indians may have possession (not full ownership) of a plot of land on the reserve—for housing, farming, and so on—if the minister allows. However, all important economic activity on reserves is subject to ministerial discretion. Moneys that are made from the sale of reserve land are managed by the minister. Wills must be approved by the minister. Local infrastructure improvements must be approved by the minister. Housing and education are at the discretion of the minister. To administer the government's directives and to allow for a modicum of local control, band council governments were established. The chief and council, who are elected every two years, act as a kind of municipal-level government subject to approval by the minister.

In setting up a reserve system and in mandating the election of local officials to oversee the administration and the implementation of federal government policy, the *Indian Act* system followed and refined the colonial system found all over the world. England, in particular, and more recently the United States, have controlled societies around the globe—Africa, the Indian subcontinent and Central America—by establishing local governments controlled by the colonizing power. As employees of the federal government, members of the band councils are in a paradoxical position. They must administer the oppressive *Indian Act* and its policies but are also the elected leaders and spokespersons for their respective communities. The National Indian Brotherhood (NIB) and the Assembly of First Nations (AFN), its successor, are made up of the *Indian Act* chiefs elected by their communities. They are the "official" leaders of their bands and the only recognized authorities in Aboriginal communities with whom the federal government will deal. Their status as *Indian Act* agents, though, has led many people in Aboriginal communities to question their capacity to speak for the people.

Gerald Alfred (1995) has argued that differing attitudes towards the band council system and the implied relationship to the Canadian state constitute an important division within Aboriginal communities. In his study of Kahnawake, Alfred concluded that the key cleavages "have formed not along class or clan lines, but on the basis of opposing strategic visions toward the achievement of shared goals offered in the general ideology [of the *Great Law of Peace*]" (1995: 84). In Kahnawake, the band council has retained a large measure of legitimacy because it advocates, as do all other groups, the ultimate rejection of the *Indian Act* and the rebirth of the Iroquois Confederacy. Despite this, there are important segments within the community that advocate the expulsion from the League of all who take part in the *Indian Act* band council. The Warrior Society, famous for its militancy during the Oka crisis, follows the teaching of the *Great Law of Peace* that no chief may "seek to establish any authority independent of the jurisdiction of the League of the Great Peace" (Wampum 25). They reject outright the legitimacy of the band council (Karoniaktajeh n.d.: 22).

Alfred summarizes the conflicting attitudes to the *Indian Act* Council:

> There is a clear distinction between the two major functions the band council performs. On the one hand, Mohawks see much potential in the further improvement of the administrative institution housed in the council office. At the same time they reject the legitimacy of the political institution centred around the council table.
>
> In a recent survey, 62% of the respondents answered "no" to the question, "Do you consider Kahnawake's existing band council structure (MCK) to be an appropriate and workable form of government for the community?" But 71% answered "yes" to the question, "Do you think it is possible to reform Kahnawake's existing band council structure (MCK) to make it an appropriate and workable form of government for the community?" (1995: 91–92)

So, while the band council and its umbrella organization, the AFN, lack legitimacy because they are seen as instruments of the Canadian state, they are the only organized voices for status Indians across the country. Thus, there exists the current ironic situation that agents of the Canadian state are currently negotiating with Canada on behalf of status Indians for the implementation of a right to self-government that is understood to be inherent.

The imposition of an alien system of elections and chiefs was not the only assimilationist policy attempted by the federal government. The history of the relationship between the Canadian state and Aboriginal peoples and communities is replete with examples of policies that have attempted to transform what is Aboriginal into what is "modern." One of the first was the outlawing of traditional spiritual practices. Beginning with first contact, the European invaders sought to weaken Aboriginal resistance by challenging its spirituality. At first, of course, the Jesuits attempted to convert Aboriginal peoples. After the passage of the *Indian Act*, other efforts were made, most notorious of which was making it an imprisonable offence to practise the Sundance.

Better known is the policy of establishing residential schools, which reached its peak in the decades from 1930 to 1960. The federal government exercised its constitutional responsibility to provide for Indian education by constructing residential schools and contracting various religious organizations to run them. The stated purpose of the schools was to provide language and skills training that would make it easier for young Indian men and women to enter the "mainstream" society's workforce. Before the residential school system was established, literacy rates were low on reserves and Aboriginal languages were usually the language of the home. Furthermore, the reserves had turned out to be refuges for the protection and transmission of traditional cultures; confining most status Indians to isolated communities insulated traditional cultures and languages from outside pressure. To break the hold of tradition and to assist in assimilation the government decided to send children off-reserve for their education. Although some fondly remember their experiences and have profited from their education, and although some parents were supportive of the education being offered their children, the majority of children and the communities themselves met with devastating results (Dyck 1997: 9–15).

Noel Dyck (1997: 14) has argued in his study of residential schools in Prince Albert that

> federal Indian administration set out to rid Indians of their languages, cultures and social identities. A set of specialized institutions, administrative practices and regulations were created to transform Indians from members of Aboriginal cultures and communities into isolated individuals who could be readily assimilated into the new society with little or no lingering trace of their cultural ancestry.
>
> Within this approach Indian schooling was engineered, first and foremost, to advance the objective of cultural assimilation.
>
> The residential school was the key institution for promoting assimilation. It was designed to separate Indian children from their families so they could be systematically fitted with the religious beliefs, social habits and educational training that would turn them into "brown white men."

A disturbing and inspiring first-hand account of the residential schools is Isabelle Knockwood's *Out of the Depths* (1992). In it she describes her experiences at the Indian residential school in Shubenacadie from 1936 to 1947. Despite moments of sharing with other children and of comradeship and compassion, the years at Shubenacadie left deep scars on many, including Isabelle. Her first memory of the school was the day of her arrival at age 5.

> Mom asked, "Tami theyarvin?" [Where are you from?] and the girl responded, "Red Bank." The nun shifted her weight and Mom looked puzzled but didn't say anything more. She had no way of predicting that within a year's time, her own four children would be behaving in the same manner when spoken to in Mi'Kmaw. Right off, Sister Mary Leonard began to explain that speaking Mi'Kmaw was not permitted in the school because it held children back in the classroom in reading, pronouncing and writing English. My parents wanted their children to succeed in school and they trusted the educators. (Knockwood 1992: 26)

Speaking Mi'kmaw could result in a beating or in being deprived of food. The universal experience of the children at Shubenacadie was that their Native language was lost.

Under the *Indian Act*, the power of the Indian agents, those authorized to run the reserves, is immense. Sections 114–23 of the Act empower the minister to operate schools on- and off-reserve for Indian children. In addition, Indian agents are empowered to enforce attendance. Acting as a truant officer, the agent may:

> enter any place where he believes, on reasonable grounds, that there are Indian children who are between the ages of seven and sixteen years, or who are required by the Minister to attend school.
>
> A truant officer [also] may take into custody a child whom he believes on reasonable grounds to be absent from school contrary to this Act and may convey the child to school, using as much force as the circumstances require. (Section 119)

Knockwood (1992: 114–15) quotes a letter dated January 1939 from C.A. Spinney, Indian agent, to the Department of Indian Affairs.

> Dear Sir:
>
> The Indians here in Cambridge Reserve were determined to have their children who are attending the Shubenacadie Indian School-home during the xmas vacation.
>
> I refused to grant their request and advised them that this was against the rules of the Dept. These people went so far as [to] have a man go to the school for their children. They did not get the children. Father Mackey would not let them take the children.
>
> This Mrs. Nibby who you had the letter from thought by writing she would be able to get her children home for xmas.

> These people think they can have their own way and would like to do so[,] and when they find out they cannot they get mad. I had your rules and regulations regarding this matter.

Beatings and abuse, including sexual abuse, were common. Especially difficult was the isolation from one's family, community and culture. It took years for Isabelle Knockwood to rediscover her identity and sense of self. Children who had finished their schooling graduated to a world that seemed alien to them no matter where they turned. Despite their European education, the prevalence of racism in Canadian society left them as outsiders. Equally difficult was the return home after having lost their language and often even their respect for traditional culture. Many communities are still struggling with the aftermath of this fracture in the continuity of their culture. Knowledge of their languages has been lost to a significant degree, as has knowledge of customs and traditions. Alien goals and ideologies were introduced that conflicted with traditional values. Most damaging of all was the fact that two generations grew up without the benefit of positive parental role models. Many people speak of this as the worst effect of the residential schools. Children had little or no contact with guardians who acted in a loving and nurturing way.

The White Paper and Its Aftermath

Federal government attempts to assimilate Aboriginals and to abolish Aboriginal culture came to a head in 1969 when Minister of Indian Affairs Jean Chrétien introduced the now infamous White Paper. This proposed bill advocated the abolition of the *Indian Act* and with it Indian status; Indians on reserves were to be encouraged to leave their communities and move to cities or towns and enter the "mainstream" workforce. Reserves were notoriously poor and Indians were the poorest, least educated, shortest lived, most poorly housed segment of the population. They suffered from enormously high levels of unemployment. In 1970, the average age at death for Indians was 42 years; for Canada as a whole it was 66 years. In 1971, only 34.7 percent of those over 15 years of age living on reserves were in the labour force. In 1969 only 12.6 percent of the on-reserve population finished high school. In 1968 less than 30 percent of homes on reserves had running water (Frideres 1998: Chapter 5). Many saw the *Indian Act* and the paternalism and heavy-handed control exercised over reserve communities as a significant contributor to the desperate conditions under which most Indians lived.

However, for most status Indians the elimination of legal differentiation and status was not an appropriate answer to their poverty and oppression. Ironically, although the *Indian Act* had been intended as a means of controlling the Aboriginal population for the ultimate purpose of assimilation, it preserved traditional culture, in part at least, by insulating Aboriginal communities from the influences of much of modernity. Where previous regimes had sought to abolish Aboriginal culture through isolation and "re-education" in the manner of concentration camps, Trudeau and Chrétien proposed to assimilate by forced integration. The White Paper was given a very hostile reception by most Indian leaders, who understood its implications for the continued survival of Aboriginal life in Canada. It eventually was withdrawn. In fact, it served as a catalyst both to stimulate greater organizational and lobbying efforts by Aboriginal groups and to raise consciousness of and pride in Aboriginal culture and heritage.

We can briefly review the critical facts of the relationship between the federal government and Aboriginal peoples in the years following the White Paper, as these facts are well-known. The watershed date in this more recent relationship was April 17, 1982, when the *Charter of Rights and Freedoms* was added to the Canadian constitution. When the first ministers began their deliberations Aboriginal issues (and, indeed, women's issues) were not on the table. Intense lobbying by the National Indian Brotherhood led to inclusion of Sections 25 and 35 in the new *Charter.*

> 25. The guarantee in this Charter of certain rights and freedoms shall not be construed so as to abrogate or derogate from any aboriginal, treaty or other rights or freedoms that pertain to the aboriginal peoples of Canada including
>
> (a) any rights or freedoms that have been recognized by the Royal Proclamation of October 7, 1763; and
>
> (b) any rights or freedoms that may be acquired by the aboriginal peoples of Canada by way of land claims settlement.
>
> 35. (1) The existing aboriginal and treaty rights of the aboriginal peoples of Canada are hereby recognized and affirmed.
>
> (2) In this Act, "aboriginal peoples of Canada" includes the Indian, Inuit and Métis peoples of Canada.

This victory was important for two reasons. First, it precipitated significant consequences, especially for Aboriginal women. Second, it further enhanced the sense of identity and pride that had developed as a result of the successful fight to scrap the White Paper.

However, the promise of a new round of constitutional negotiations that would deal exclusively with Aboriginal issues, particularly the difficult one of self-government, eventually came to nought. Were Aboriginal peoples Canadian citizens, subject to the sovereignty of the Crown and part of the multicultural mosaic; or were they international actors, tied to Canada through treaties and other international agreements? What were Canada's obligations under the treaties to provide access to land and resources? What degree of autonomy was acceptable to both sides? After five years of conferences and negotiations, no answers to these questions were forthcoming.

Shortly after these negotiations failed, the Meech Lake Accord was signed. Designed to "bring Quebec back in" after its rejection of the 1982 constitutional amendments, the Meech Lake Accord neglected to mention Aboriginal peoples. The outrage of Aboriginal groups at this perceived slight accounted in part for the failure of the Accord; Elijah Harper, a member of Manitoba's legislative assembly and a status Indian, helped scuttle the Accord by delaying the vote past the required date for passage. When the federal government made a second attempt to satisfy Quebec's demands in the 1992 Charlottetown Accord, it did not make the same mistake. Section 41–56 of this new Accord included the promise of constitutionalizing the Aboriginal demand for self-government and, particularly, expanding the notion of treaty and Aboriginal rights to include the right to self-government.

> 41. *The Inherent Right of Self-Government*
>
> The Constitution should be amended to recognize that the Aboriginal peoples of Canada have the inherent right of self-government within Canada. This right should be placed in a new section of the *Constitution Act, 1982*, Section 35.1(1).
>
> The recognition of the inherent right of self-government should be interpreted in light of the recognition of Aboriginal governments as one of three orders of government in Canada.
>
> A contextual statement should be inserted in the Constitution, as follows:
>
> "The exercise of the right of self-government includes the authority of the duly constituted legislative bodies of Aboriginal peoples, each within its own jurisdiction:
>
> (a) to safeguard and develop their languages, cultures, economies, identities, institutions and traditions; and,
>
> b) to develop, maintain and strengthen their relationship with their lands, waters and environment
>
> so as to determine and control their development as peoples according to their own values and priorities and ensure the integrity of their societies.

Over the years the desire for justice and the preservation of traditional life have, for many, coalesced around the demand for self-government. The paternalism of the *Indian Act* and the continued memory of the autonomy exercised by Aboriginal societies before being overwhelmed by Europeans have led to the articulation of a variety of complex and sometimes contradictory yearnings under the heading of "self-government." As many critics have pointed out, however, self-government is a vague concept. Tom Flanagan, for instance, who supports the abolitionist policy of the White Paper, has written that

> realism must intervene at some point. We are talking about six hundred bands with an average population of less than a thousand, mostly living on small, remote pieces of land without significant job opportunities, natural resources or economic prospects.... How are such small, isolated, and impoverished groups of people supposed to support and operate an untried system of government incorporating a degree of complexity not seen since the medieval Holy Roman Empire? (1998: 11)

It is probably fair to say that the federal government's notion of self-government and the Aboriginal understanding of the idea are very different. The federal government does not interpret self-government as involving any ceding of sovereignty on its part. Self-government, as it is being implemented, for example, in the Sechelt band, means that local, municipal-style government is being established in reserve communities (Etkin 1988: 74). Bands will administer education, health services, housing and other local services. This is far removed from the demands for sovereignty contained in the self-government proposals of the Mohawk communities in Quebec and Ontario, however. While reserve communities differ on their desired degree of autonomy, it is likely that most want more authority than the federal government is prepared to give.

The degree to which many status Indians do not consider themselves primarily as Canadian, and the extent of their self-identification apart from the Canadian ethnic mosaic, can be seen in their responses to central features of citizenship, such as voting. F. Laurie Barron's (1997) study of the CCF policies regarding Indians and Métis in Saskatchewan under Premier Tommy Douglas is revealing. Attempting to alleviate the terrible poverty of reserves, Douglas proposed to integrate Indians and Métis into the economic mainstream through a number of measures. Critical, though, was eliminating their second-class citizen status under federal and provincial law. According to the *Dominion Elections Act*, status Indians could not vote in federal elections prior to 1960. This was the case in all provinces except Nova Scotia, whose restrictions on Indian voting rights made exercise of the franchise difficult. Douglas wanted to change Saskatchewan's voting law so that status Indians could vote. Interestingly, the majority of Indians were opposed "because they believed it entailed a loss of treaty rights" (Barron 1997: 100).

In 1960 the federal government of John Diefenbaker revised the *Elections Act* so that Indians could vote and not lose their status. By 1962 most provinces had followed suit. A study of Indian voter participation in the Maritimes by David Bedford and Sidney Pobihushchy (1995: 269–70) reveals some interesting trends. At first voter participation was quite high. The 1962 federal election, the first after the change to the electoral laws, saw turnout rates of 70 percent for New Brunswick and 89.3 percent for Nova Scotia. By 1988 voter turnout had dropped to 17.8 percent for New Brunswick and 54 percent for Nova Scotia. Provincial election results tell the same story. Voter turnout in the 1967 New Brunswick election was 64.4 percent. By 1991 the number had sunk to 27.6 percent. Nova Scotia's 1967 provincial election turnout for status Indians was 67.2 percent, in 1993 it was 45.2 percent. Bedford and Pobihushchy proposed that none of the usual socio-demographic factors could explain the remarkable decline and that the likely cause of decreasing participation in elections was a withdrawal of legitimacy. Simply put, "Indians" were increasingly seeing their primary identity as Mi'kmaw or Maliseet rather than as Canadian citizens (Bedford and Pobihushchy 1995: 269–70).

The rejection of their identity as Canadian and the retention of an Aboriginal identity leads to an important, and as yet unresolved, problematic. Self-governing Aboriginal communities that wish to preserve an Aboriginal identity and culture must face the question that Aristotle argued all communities must face: "how to live well." In this case the issue is compounded because what it means to be Aboriginal in the new millennium is not at all clear. As Gerald Alfred (1995) has pointed out, there are divisions in communities based on strategies for achieving common goals. In many communities there is also conflict over what goals to pursue. The question of "how to live well Aboriginally" is almost by necessity extraordinarily difficult to answer.

Two separate sets of questions must be answered before this guiding issue of practical wisdom, of politics, can be answered. The first set of questions deals with how a traditional culture based on a non-modern political economy can be maintained in an era when capitalism is penetrating into the remotest areas of the world. Even the Aboriginal peoples of the Brazilian rain forest are in danger of losing their culture. How do communities negotiate the "in-betweenness" of present Aboriginal life and consciousness? How do they unite the often contradictory demand to reject modernity and yet embrace it? They are often caught between two cultural poles which are incompatible, but each compelling. The second set of questions acknowledges that, even if the first set of questions can be answered, there remains the problem of establishing an adequate relationship with the Canadian state. Can this be done without a significant transformation to the Canadian state itself?

The tension that Aboriginal peoples experience between the seemingly incommensurate social worlds of traditional life and modern capitalist society presents great challenges for Marxist analysis. Hints at the recognition of this difficulty can be found in the writings of Marx and Engels themselves. They are also present in the practical and theoretical articulations of contemporary left groups and intellectuals. Is Marxism, as a social, revolutionary movement, committed to advancing the essential properties of modernity? Is it committed to the enlightenment notion that history is the story of the progress of human society, with progress defined as increasing technological capacity to transform nature? Is capitalism, especially the process of its universalization, necessary for the advent of the social relations of communism? Is Marxism's understanding of human beings such that there can be value in preserving traditional cultures? There is little doubt that the historical and contemporary Canadian state and the capitalist economy of Canada have had little to offer Aboriginal peoples except assimilation. There is also little doubt that this assimilation—whether it be benign, as in the attraction of the consumer lifestyle, or forced, as in the oppression of the residential school system—has been resisted, less successfully sometimes, more successfully at other times. Can Marxist thought and those inspired by it offer anything of value to this struggle?

CHAPTER 2

ABORIGINAL GENOCIDE AND THE LEFT

The goal of this chapter is not a historical reconstruction of the development of ideas and policies of the left with regard to Aboriginal issues. Such an investigation for all of the left is beyond the scope of this book. Rather, we are attempting to present views typical of the left in sufficient detail that:

- their understanding of the causes and nature of the oppression of Aboriginal peoples can be unpacked;
- the reading or interpretation of Marx, which underlies their analysis, can be brought to the surface;
- differences, if any, between the various left groups and intellectuals can be discerned; and
- judgement can be passed on the adequacy of their understandings of the present relationship between Aboriginal peoples and the dominant society.

Just as Aboriginal peoples and cultures do not constitute a single, monolithic reality, so it is that what we call the "left" is an ambiguous collection of varying groups and thinkers. For the purposes of this study the analyses and policies of the following four parties, groups and individuals will be examined.

The Canadian Commonwealth Federation (after 1961 the New Democratic Party) was founded in 1933 in western Canada by farmers, workers and intellectuals. While non-Marxist, the Canadian Commonwealth Federation (CCF) argued in its founding document, the *Regina Manifesto*, that the current economic system of private ownership and profiteering and the concomitant exploitation of workers and small producers must be replaced. Further, it argued that a system of cooperatively- and publicly-owned enterprises must replace the corporate domination of the economy. By 1961 the CCF was reformed as the New Democratic Party (NDP), which had more direct organizational ties with the union movement. The NDP embraced Keynesian economic and social policies, de-emphasizing the creation of a cooperative economy and stressing more the goals common to social-democratic parties—progressive taxation, welfare, unemployment insurance, workers' safety and health care.

The Communist Party of Canada is the largest of the avowedly Marxist parties in Canada. The CPC was founded in 1921 and at various times attracted support among the urban working class. It has elected members of Parliament and has had important influence in sections of the union movement.

In addition to the Communist Party of Canada, there are other overtly Marxist groups that follow the teachings of the Russian revolutionary, Leon Trotsky. Generally smaller than the CPC, these groups—the International Socialists, the Trotskyist League of Canada and the Communist League/ Young Socialists—all have vigorous presses, which comment on and analyze the events of the day.

Finally, there are intellectuals who constitute an important part of the left milieu in Canada. Critics and commentators such as Stanley Ryerson and George Woodcock, among others, have helped both to shape the public discourse in Canada on a number of issues and to define the left perspective on important public policy questions.

The Canadian Commonwealth Federation/ New Democratic Party

Most of the public pronouncements on the Aboriginal question by the CCF/NDP originate from the period after 1961 when the party had changed to the NDP, and so this period will be our primary focus. Of course, even with this limitation, unequivocal statements regarding NDP policies involve a degree of falsification. The political groups that we will look at have changing and ambivalent understandings of these complex questions. We paint only a general picture.

The *Regina Manifesto* spoke of the need to be respectful of minority groups and cultures:

> The new social order at which we aim is not one in which individuality will be crushed out by a system of regimentation. Nor shall we interfere with cultural rights of racial or religious minorities. What we seek is a proper collective organization of our economic resources and such as will make possible … full economic, political and religious liberty for all. (Hendrickson 1976: 6)

This general orientation of respect for cultural differences and recognition of the need to temper the power of the majority in a democracy with recognition of the rights of the minority to preserve their differences is integral to CCF/NDP policy through to the present. How they have understood the implementation of this right and what they have perceived to be the main impediments to its existence will be the focus of the remainder of this section. Our goal in this and in the succeeding discussions of the other left groups will not be to present a full account of their positions on the various issues affecting Aboriginal persons. Instead, we will focus on the issue of how, if at all, Aboriginal peoples can exist as Aboriginal in the context of Canadian society.

This is a long-standing problematic for political theorists, especially in an era of liberal–democratic societies. John Stuart Mill raised concerns about the effects that majoritarian democratic politics may have on the rights of the individual to live in non-conformity with the values and standards of her or his fellow citizens. The American *Bill of Rights* and the Canadian *Charter of Rights and Freedoms* address the fears that majorities, even democratically elected ones, may abuse the rights of individual persons. Of even longer standing concern for political thinkers has been the question of minority groups. There has been much greater consensus on the appropriate means for protecting the rights of the individual than there has been on the preservation of the rights of minorities. Various mechanisms have been employed over the centuries to integrate cultural, linguistic and religious groups into a wider political structure. Empires from the Persian and Roman through to the modern period have had to face the question of how to rule disparate groups.

The very federal structure of the Canadian political system was designed to provide a jurisdictional space within which a minority religious and linguistic group could feel secure from the power of the majority. Federalism, and the concomitant jurisdictional division of powers, was constructed as an institutional solution to the question of minority group rights. Less formal, non-institutional practices, such as multicultural policies, are similarly intended to provide minority cultures with some measure of insulation from the dominant group.

Separate religious and linguistic school systems are examples of such arrangements. The specific policy question regarding a minority culture becomes what to do with their difference. First, should this difference be maintained? Should steps be taken to preserve the distinctness of the minority's culture or should an assimilationist policy—a policy that seeks to remove the cultural difference—be put into place? For example, if a minority speaking a different language exists, should the viability and use of this language be encouraged or discouraged? Second, if cultural differences are to be encouraged, how are the rights and cultural practices of the minority best maintained? Does this preservation necessitate institutional insulation, ranging in degree from complete secession to various federal arrangements? Can the cultural distinctness be preserved informally, using initiatives such as separate schools, control over the administration of programs such as health care, welfare, housing and so on?

As we will see in discussing the NDP response to these questions, and the responses of the other groups and theorists as well, the specific positions taken depend upon their analysis of two issues. The first can be called the national question. Do Aboriginal peoples, in this case, have the right to national self-determination? Are they, in fact, nations? Can they secede from Canada and create a separate, independent jurisdiction? Is their incorporation into the Canadian state inevitable? Were they independent nations before contact, and do they retain this autonomy? The second is the issue of the viability of traditional Aboriginal culture. Have the traditional cultures been irrevocably transformed? Is a viable traditional culture possible in the context of modern, technologically intense capitalist (or socialist) society? Are such cultures worthy of preservation?

The NDP understanding of these issues and questions was conditioned both by a respect for the values of traditional Aboriginal culture and by an admission of the terrible price paid by Aboriginal peoples as the result of contact. In a 1960s article in the *Commonwealth*, the official organ of the party, traditional practices were described as "a way of life more conducive to human happiness than anything the white man had to offer" (Biesick 1966: 8). The article speculates on what North America would have become if, instead of European civilization, Aboriginal civilization had dominated,

> [if] the Indians' philosophy that the world and all that is in it exists for the benefit of all—if they had built a society based on the common ownership of the means of existence—if they had established a society based on co-operation for the common goal instead of competition for selfish gain. (Biesick 1966: 9)

This theme, that traditional culture was socialist and that its destruction constitutes a loss to be lamented, is found throughout NDP publications (Wuttunee 1968: 7). Related to it is the concern that Aboriginal peoples have suffered terrible injustices at the hands of European society. The deplorable living conditions, poverty and poor health of Aboriginal peoples are results not only of individual acts of cruelty or greed but, more importantly, the inevitable consequence of the imposition of the capitalist system of private ownership (Biesick 1966: 8–9).

For the most part, however, NDP spokespersons and policy statements emphasized that while past treatment of Aboriginal persons had been horrendous, the possibility lay open for greater integration into the Canadian mainstream. The practices of previous governments had been oppressive and paternalistic. The *Indian Act* gave unreasonable power to the Minister of Indian Affairs, and legitimate land claims had been denied. Furthermore, the resources that Aboriginal communities needed to survive were being taken away. While Aboriginal communities must be given the choice to integrate or not, the NDP's clear preference was for integration. The resolutions of the NDP's 1966 Saskatchewan Provincial Convention stated:

> The larger society has room for many races, creeds and cultures. New opportunities must be seen, not as submerging traditional Indian culture, but as a means to a more abundant life in which can be kept what is wanted from the past.... Because most jobs are in Saskatchewan cities, there is urgent need for progress in the urban centres which can help the Indian adjust to the new environment, to a different type and rhythm of work and to a whole new way of life. (*Prairie New Democrat Commonwealth* 1966: 5)

This ambivalence between a disinclination to force integration and a recognition that the realities of the modern economy are such that traditional life is not really an option runs throughout NDP analysis. A 1970 convention resolution in Ontario stated that "the NDP accepts as a basic principle the right of Native people to self-determination and self-preservation" (Hendrickson 1976: 6); and yet, just three years before, Tommy Douglas said in a speech in the House of Commons: "We all hope the day will come in Canada when the Indian people will have received sufficient education and will have been absorbed into the mainstream of Canadian life" (Douglas 1967: 8).

A speech that Douglas gave in Peace River, Alberta, in June 1968 cogently expressed the tension in NDP thinking between the right of Aboriginal peoples to determine their own future and the overwhelming constraints placed on the practice of this right by modern realities. After summarizing the dispiriting history of the relationship between Canada and the Aboriginal peoples of Turtle Island, Douglas proposed the following measures to change this past relationship:

> First, Indians must manage their own affairs. The *Indian Act* needs to be totally re-written removing any paternalistic elements. The Indian Affairs Branch must increase its staff, making provision for

> responsible positions for Indians. More powers of self-government must be held by the reserve; giving the reserve municipal status should be considered in consultation with Indians.
>
> Second, development of the resources on the Indians' land must be carried out under the direction of Indians but with the necessary material and technical know how being made available to them. Capital must be made available for the establishment of co-operative industries.
>
> Third, education opportunities for Indians must be improved. The first step would be to design course material which takes into account the difference in the Indian cultural background. Indians must be provided with the skills to make their way in our industrialized society. (Douglas 1968: 8)

Similar statements from the 1960s to the 1980s stress the need for greater access to education, programs to encourage employment opportunities and affirmative action initiatives to allow for greater self-regulation of reserve communities.

What emerges from Douglas' speech is the normalization of the economy and technology of modern society. That the Canadian economy will continue to be in its main features what it has always been is simply taken for granted. Unlike the CPC and the Trotskyist parties, who tie Aboriginal liberation to fundamental changes in the forms of property ownership, the NDP's position means reforming the current system to make a space in it for equitable Aboriginal participation. It looks to changes in government practice—reforms to the *Indian Act*; affirmative action programs to allow for greater Aboriginal participation in decision-making; increased spending on health, education and housing; and, finally, removal of the barriers to full Aboriginal participation in Canadian political, social and economic life—as the means to normalize Aboriginal status in Canadian life. The NDP analysis of the "Aboriginal question" focuses on racism as the general name for the myriad of factors that inhibit participation in mainstream life. Of course, this narrowing of focus still leaves plenty to talk about. The litany of expressions of racism is almost unfathomably long. Such a concentration, however, does mean that issues critical to Aboriginal understanding of their own situation are not fully addressed. This includes, above all, the issues of national sovereignty and the preservation of traditional culture.

The concept of culture implicit in the NDP policies and analysis further reveals the source of the party's failure to come to terms with these critical issues. The preservation of culture is understood as the maintenance of language, spirituality, family relationships and so on; it does not refer primarily to the material culture of traditional societies. NDP policies assume that integration into the modern economy is inevitable and good, so the real incommensurability of modern and traditional cultures is never brought to the surface. Instead, it is hoped that Aboriginals will still be able to speak their language at home, drum and chant, even though they will be participating in Western education and in a modern economy.

The Communist Party of Canada

Unlike the NDP, which has its intellectual and theoretical roots in Marx, Fabian socialists, the cooperative movement, Christian Socialism and so on, the CPC is an overtly Marxist party. It is influenced overwhelmingly by the writings of Karl Marx and Friedrich Engels and by the writings and actions of V.I. Lenin and Josef Stalin. The greater consistency of the sources of its policies means that the policies themselves are more logically coherent than those of the NDP. Despite this, however, the respective understandings of the Aboriginal question display some surprising similarities. Most notable, as we will see, is the tension, common to both, between a commitment to some degree of Aboriginal self-determination and the acceptance that this right is severely constrained in practice by the consequences of the march of technological progress.

In the CPC journal *Communist Viewpoint*, Ben Swankey argued that it is

> essential that the socialist and labor movements take up the cause of the native peoples with more vigor than ever. As the victims of the policies of our era of monopoly capitalism, the native peoples are the natural allies of labor. Helping to raise their wages and living standards will raise those of labor. Helping them defeat discrimination and achieve equality will help to eradicate prejudices that have rubbed off and persist in some sections of labor. (1969: 53)

It is important to note the basis for Swankey's "natural alliance" between labour and Native peoples. Both groups undergo the same exploitation and experience the same oppression; that is, the alliance is predicated on a common experience as workers in a capitalist economy. Furthermore, common cause must be made under the leadership of the working-class movements (Fletcher 1981: 45). Compare this to the related view of the New Democratic Party, which saw in the traditional culture of Aboriginal peoples an anticipation of the values of cooperation and reciprocal exchange and which the NDP wants to see replace competitive capitalist relations.

When one examines the statements of the CPC on the nature of pre-contact Aboriginal societies a consistent picture emerges. *Canada's Party of Socialism: The History of the Communist Party of Canada, 1921–1976*, the

CPC's official accounting of their history and policies, states that, when the Europeans first arrived in Canada,

> they found a sparsely populated country that was already occupied by distinct peoples who spoke many different languages and stood at varying levels of economic and social development. For some of these peoples, agriculture formed the basis of tribal life, but for most, subsistence was sustained through hunting and fishing. (Communist Party of Canada 1982: 271–72)

They were less developed technologically and in terms of material culture than the Europeans, and this disparity led to their easy defeat at the hands of the newcomers. The arrival of the Europeans "interrupted the independent historical development of the Native peoples" (Communist Party of Canada 1982: 222) and unleashed a terrible oppression upon them, which continues to the present.

The CPC's evaluation of Aboriginal cultures, in terms of a scale of historical development determined by the "stage" of the material culture, presages their complex and ambiguous understanding of the national question and its relation to ideas of progress and historical evolution. While the CPC accepts the right of Aboriginal peoples to self-determination and to participation in decisions affecting their communities, it stops short of recognizing their full right to autonomy and independence. Their reason for advocating only limited rights to self-government is their view that Aboriginal peoples do not qualify as "nations." The CPC, like all organizations that claim Lenin as a founding theorist, argues that "national" groups must have the right to full self-determination, including the right to separate or secede if so desired. However, the CPC argues that, because they are without a common language or shared economic life, Aboriginal peoples do not constitute nations. Then party leader William Kashtan wrote:

> As for the Indian and Inuit people, in a strictly scientific sense they are not presently nations, although they could, under certain circumstances, become so. They have no common language, economic life or territory, spread over, as they are, in many parts of the country, as single local communities. As nations they would have, as a matter of course, the right to national self-determination up to and including secession. Because they do not constitute nations, the Communist Party program—*The Road to Socialism in Canada*—speaks of their right to national identity and development of their culture. This includes full respect for their autonomy, with regard

> to regional self-government, their land claims, culture, language, education, and not least, a voice in determining economic development and its fruits, in the areas they occupy, based on full power of decision-making on all questions pertaining to their affairs as Native Peoples. (1977: 7)

In place of full recognition of national rights, the CPC proposes self-determination concerning matters pertaining to their unique culture as well as the promise of enhanced incorporation into the mainstream economy.

> A socialist Canada will take meaningful measures to compensate the Native Peoples for the historical injustices perpetrated upon them by the British and French colonizers of Canada and continued under the rule of monopoly capital. Such measures will include full recognition of their national identity and development of their Native cultures; full power of decision-making on all questions pertaining to their affairs as Native Peoples; the rooting out of all vestiges of racism and discrimination; full equality before the law and in society; a massive economic and social program to bring their living, health, housing and education standards, training and job opportunities up to accepted Canadian standards. The Indian and Inuit peoples will enjoy regional self-government and full rights to their language and culture. (Communist Party of Canada 1977: 62)

Preservation of traditional material culture is not a practical policy option for the CPC. *The Road to Socialism in Canada* (Communist Party of Canada 1977) further articulates the party's understanding of history and of the forces that shape it. Socialism naturally follows from capitalism, as the latter inevitably suffers from internal contradictions and the inability to provide abundance for everyone. "Socialism," it is argued, "is the logical next step in our country's historical development" because only socialism "can successfully meet the challenge of such new productive powers as automation, electronics, cybernetics, and nuclear energy" (Communist Party of Canada 1977: 1–2). Socialism is able, as capitalism is not, to employ the continually improving technologies of production for everyone's benefit, "no longer restricted by the anarchy, waste, wars and economic crises of the profit system, [hence] the productive capacity will expand enormously and the living standards of the Canadian people will rise accordingly" (Communist Party of Canada 1977: 1). This new abundance will result from the more efficient and socially beneficial use of technology under socialism.

> Peaceful use of nuclear energy and further development of automation will transform industrial techniques. Giant projects based on over-all planning will change the economic map of Canada. This will transform and develop our great Northern regions and eliminate regional disparities created by monopoly rule. (Communist Party of Canada 1977: 58)

Further, the working class will labour hard in developing and expanding productive capacities and, "motivated by the knowledge that every increase in production goes to the benefit of society as a whole and themselves as individuals, will quickly and continually increase the amount of the total national product" (Communist Party of Canada 1977: 58–59).

The CPC takes a cautionary tone regarding the increased productive capabilities that result from technological development. Such improvements contribute, for example, to higher unemployment under capitalist relations of productions. However, the worrisome consequences are overcome when such techniques are applied under socialist relations.

> The revolution in science and technology has not only aggravated all the former contradictions of capitalism—it has engendered new ones. The most acute social problem is unemployment, which will become a more serious problem as industry enters a higher stage of automation. This trend will continue and will sharpen social conflicts. The fundamental solution is not to limit or hinder technological development but to change capitalist private relations of production into social relations, with the working people thereby becoming the beneficiaries of the revolution in science and technology. (Communist Party of Canada 1977: 14)

Two points stand out when the CPC's policies on the right of self-determination for Aboriginal peoples are considered together with their commitment to the necessity and beneficence of increasing technological mastery. First, the implied vision of the good life for all people is one of increased production and consumption. Aboriginal rights to self-determination are conditioned by this superceding value. Limits on national rights make sense if greater consumption is, in fact, a ubiquitous human value. If it is a culturally specific value, however, applying it to all peoples is a form chauvinism, even if well-intentioned. It is clear, for example, from the importance of the ethic of sharing, that maximizing consumption was not an important value for Aboriginal peoples. Second, supporting rights to cultural autonomy within a broader economy committed to maximizing production reveals that the CPC, like the NDP, understands culture to refer to the non-material aspects of a people's life. That is, culture is language, spirituality, family relations, attitudes and morals and so on, *not* the social relations and modes of production. This is a somewhat surprising position to be taken by a party that is explicit about its indebtedness to Marx, and this position is inconsistent with the CPC's analysis of the inevitable replacement of traditional economies with modern ones. Marx argued that, although aspects of life such as language, family arrangements and spirituality, affect economic relations, they cannot continue to exist independent of these relations. Aboriginal respect for the land, for example, cannot be expected to continue when all are working in factories that pollute the air, land and water. Whether such aspects of culture as language and spiritual values can be sustained in any meaningful way in the absence of a flourishing traditional material culture is an unanswered, yet critical, question.

Trotskyist Groups

The left also includes a number of smaller parties that explicitly follow the teachings of Marx and Lenin but that are critical of the Communist Party of Canada and its long-standing affiliation with the policies of the Union of Soviet Socialist Republics. The CPC was a member of the Moscow-dominated Third International, and it supported the actions of Stalin and subsequent Soviet leaders. The International Socialists (IS), the Trotskyist League of Canada (TLC) and the Communist League/Young Socialists (CL/YS), which are the Canadian branches of international organizations, are all Marxist parties but critical of the domestic and foreign policies of the former Soviet Union. They are much smaller than the CPC, but nonetheless influential among the left in Canada because of their rigorous presses and public actions, such as participation in demonstrations and so on. While there are differences between the groups, even on the Aboriginal question, for our purposes we shall see that on certain key issues there is important agreement.

The three parties share common ground on two critical points. First, all argue that the ultimate source or cause of the oppression of Aboriginal peoples is the system of capitalist economic relations. It is not the industrial system or the intensification of technology, but the private ownership of property that lies at the root of the problems experienced by Aboriginal persons. The CL/YS paper, the *Militant*, wrote that "the oppression of the native peoples stems entirely from the development of capitalism in Canada" (Dugre and Simms 1990: 10). Similarly, we can find argued in the IS paper, the *Socialist Worker,* that capitalism in Canada

> is a system committed to protecting its property from the inherent rights of native people. Canada is a nation borne of conquest. Native peoples ... were conquered, their land and rights stolen

> from them, in order to secure from coast to coast the basis of what is today the federal Canadian state. (1997: 3)

We shall see that such an analysis of the cause of oppression, namely the system of ownership, results in arguments by all three groups that the only possible solution to the problem of oppression is socialist revolution—a radical transformation of the system of property ownership from private to public/collective.

In addition to the shared understanding that capitalism is the ultimate source of the difficulties facing Aboriginal peoples is the notion, common to all three groups, that the specific (and heightened) form that the exploitation of Native persons takes is conditioned by the prevalent racism of Canadian society; all who are not owners of the means of production are subject to exploitation, and some groups are especially singled out. Racism and sexism, both of which target specific groups, exist and are exacerbated under capitalism as a way of fragmenting the working-class struggle against their common enemy (the bourgeoisie) and as a means of creating pools of cheaper labour. Women, African-Canadian and Aboriginal persons are all less costly to hire than white males, in large measure because their precarious social position makes them vulnerable and desperate. Proponents of the left in general, and Trotskyist groups in particular, argue that the unique oppression experienced by Aboriginal persons, in addition to the exploitation that all in the working class undergo, is the result of a racism that is endemic to capitalism and that will be overcome only by the socialist transformation of society. There is certainly no shortage of examples regarding the racism of Canadian society, and left presses have highlighted the more egregious examples.

The solution, therefore, that these groups propose is socialist revolution. As stated in *Spartacist Canada,* the paper of the TLC, "[O]nly Socialist revolution can shatter the heavy chains of racist capitalist oppression which has dragged the Native peoples into degradation and misery, and usher in an egalitarian socialist society which can redress centuries of injustice" (1995: 11) As the experiences of Aboriginal peoples is generally the same as that of all other members of the working class, even if specifically different because of racism, the appropriate tactic in the common struggle against capitalism is the inclusion of the Aboriginal question within the broader socialist movement. That is, Aboriginal groups should be included in the more general struggle of labour against capital. "The growing incorporation of natives into the working class and into the unions has strengthened their economic independence, their self-confidence, and their capacity to fight, which are essential elements of their capacity to resist national oppression" (*Militant* 1992: 10). The focus of struggle should be around class issues because it is the "system of exploitation and oppression, not questions of 'race' or 'culture,' that are at the root of the current situation" (*Militant* 1992: 10).

The three groups are in agreement that the dynamic nature of the capitalist system has rendered the preservation of traditional Aboriginal material culture impossible. Further, the absence of such a living material culture and the geographic fragmentation of reserve communities have destroyed the Aboriginal peoples' nationhood. Traditional economic practices such as communal property ownership and sharing within clans severely restricted the possibilities of the expansion of capitalist relations across North America. Any land or resource that was held Aboriginally was not available for exploitation. The consequence was that the expansion of the Canadian state had as its primary purpose the destruction of all that was Aboriginal. This meant first of all transforming traditional forms of property, but it also included the destruction of the cultural and linguistic practices accompanying the traditional material culture. The TLC has argued that the development of capitalism and the emergence of a "modern" way of life were inevitable and that less developed cultures are doomed. Any attempts at maintaining traditional lifestyles, therefore, are completely futile.

> The options for Native people are often presented as a choice between "traditional culture" and racist capitalist society. But this is a false choice, not least because the vibrant pre-European culture is irreparably lost. The real choice is between the perpetuation of the crimes of the past—centuries of racist genocide and wholesale destruction of the Natives' way of life—or the creation of a future in a society not based on brutal exploitation and all-sided racism. We reject the idealization of "traditional culture" as liberal racism and a patronizing glorification of backwardness. (*Women and Revolution* 1993: 15)

The view held by the three groups that the historical trajectory, guided by progressive developments in the technologies of production, is necessary and unstoppable colours their positions on the national question. All are in agreement that the Canadian state has unfairly excluded Aboriginal persons from democratic participation in decision-making, and all are supportive of Aboriginal communities making their own decisions regarding their communities' political life and development. However, all fall short in arguing for autonomy or sovereignty for Aboriginal communities. The rather complex nature of their positions can be seen in the following statements by the IS and the TLC. In their *Internal Bulletin* (1996: 4), the International Socialists argue:

> Capitalism has developed unevenly, with nations divided into oppressor and oppressed. The challenge we face is breaking the bond between workers of the oppressor country with their own ruling class. Only then can we hope to break the hold of nationalism on the workers of the oppressed country, whose nationalism is a response to imperialism.
>
> Our position is unequivocal: we stand with the oppressed nations against imperialism. But we are not nationalists. We do not believe the solution to national oppression lies in a nationalist point of view, but in its opposite, internationalism.
>
> We are therefore critical of the strategies and politics adopted by nationalist movements of oppressed nations. While drawing a distinction between the nationalism of oppressor and oppressed, and supporting the latter in anti-imperialist demands, we make *no concession to the ideology of nationalism.*

More starkly, the Trotskyist League of Canada writes:

> Seeking to address their desperate situation some Native leaders speak in terms of "sovereignty" and "self-determination." But the possibility of the formation of a Native nation or nations was long ago foreclosed when the Indians' tribal societies came face to face with the advance of capitalism. "Self-determination" is therefore a utopian and potentially dangerous illusion. (*Spartacist Canada* 1990: 19)

Both positions clearly reject Native nationalism as a viable road to liberation.

Like the NDP and the CPC, the Trotskyist groups focused on the problem of racism as a critical source for the involuntary segregation of Aboriginal persons. Racist attitudes exclude peoples from integrating into the mainstream by denying them access to jobs, housing and education. The intimidation of Native persons, especially by the police, creates an unwelcoming climate off-reserve. Racism is understood as directly linked to the capitalist economic system; hence these groups anticipate that when the source of racist attitudes in the relations of production are removed by the emergence of a socialist society, the main impediment to assimilation into the dominant, modern society will disappear.

Intellectuals on the Left

The majority of Canada's leading intellectuals have paid little attention to the Aboriginal question. "Canadian identity" is much more involved with English–French relations and with carving out a space that is separate from our neighbours to the south. Even the story of the founding of Canada emphasizes these two components, along with heroic tales of settling the west, to the exclusion of almost all else. Historians like Jack Granatstein, who are self-consciously attempting to construct a distinctively Canadian identity, speak of battles on foreign lands, such as the battle at Vimy Ridge, as Canada's coming-of-age. Such histories, and there are many, are written from the perspective of the European conquerors, so much so that Aboriginal communities and cultures constitute just one more natural fact or external condition to be dealt with and overcome. Why this is so is not hard to discern. One cannot easily write the triumphant story of Canadian history and identity and still speak honestly of the destruction that its founding has meant to millions of Aboriginal people, so this part of the story is forgotten.

There have been exceptions. Stanley Ryerson wrote extensively of the Aboriginal peoples in *The Founding of Canada* (1960). One of the few widely known Canadian intellectuals to identify himself publicly as a Marxist, Ryerson drew upon Marx's historical materialism to account for Canadian development. The historian's task is to explain "the succession of social systems that have marked, one after the other, the stages of his progression" (Ryerson 1960: vii). In the earliest stages of history, humans are closely tied to nature and dependent upon its rhythms. Gradually, improvements in technologies allow for greater mastery of nature. This results in increasing separation from nature and the development of stages of history defined by the ensuing social relationships.

Ryerson's writings have been influential within the Communist Party of Canada, and his analysis helps illuminate the party's positions. He characterized the cultures of the Iroquoian–Algonkian peoples as primitive–communal; that is, organized around communal production. Property was held in common. Society was organized around extended family groupings, and there were no hierarchical divisions among the people. Levels of technique in these communities were low, as they possessed only the rudimentary tools needed to survive. Men and women expended most of their energies in providing for subsistence needs. As a consequence, there was little time to spend on improving the techniques of production (Ryerson 1960: Chapter 5).

Contact was disastrous for Aboriginal communities because it meant both the dissolution of traditional life and the concomitant incorporation into a capitalist economy. Ryerson argued that

> Indian primitive–communal society never reached the point of break up into class society as a result of its own economic development. Its normal evolution was cut short by European conquest—which disrupted tribal society and sought to impose in its place the pattern of capitalist class relations. (Ryerson 1960: 36)

The primary transmission belt for the infiltration of capitalist relations into traditional societies was the fur trade. Europeans arrived in North America at an early stage in the development of capitalism, a phase described by Marx as "primitive accumulation." During this period, capital is acquired for investment by extracting resources and labour, especially from those outside the emerging capitalist system. For example, Europeans went to Africa where they acquired slaves. These enslaved persons were then transported to the Caribbean and southern American colonies, where they toiled on plantations. The resulting commodities were sold in Europe for enormous profits.

Although the modalities were different, the fur trade was part of the same global process. European traders induced Aboriginal communities to engage in trapping and skinning for the purposes of trade. Ryerson was particularly concerned by the fact that the exchanges were unequal, at least in terms of the European economy (Ryerson 1960: 86–87, 262). Similarly, the treaties that were signed were unequal. Fraud and subterfuge meant that Aboriginal communities ceded land rights without fully realizing the consequences (Ryerson 1960: 239–41).

As Ryerson's writings often grounded the analyses of the CPC, so the writings of Thomas Berger have helped shaped the policies of the NDP. Berger, a lawyer and analyst, is best known as commissioner on the Mackenzie Valley Pipeline Inquiry. Berger considers Aboriginal peoples to be unique among Canada's minorities, not only because they are the descendants of the original inhabitants of this land but because they, unlike other minority groups, do not wish to integrate into the dominant culture. Instead, they are seeking to remain culturally and politically autonomous. They prefer to live in self-governing communities where their cultures can be preserved (Berger 1991: 82). Unlike Ryerson (and George Novack as we will see later), Berger does not believe that assimilation into Western culture and the concomitant destruction of indigenous culture are inevitable. There are critical features of Aboriginal cultures that continue to exist despite the pressures of the past five centuries. Consensus decision-making, respect for elders, the extended family structure and, especially, a spiritual respect for the land and living creatures are still integral parts of Aboriginal communities (Berger 1991: 160). These beliefs and practices can be expected to continue to exist, and they are definitive of the Aboriginal worldview.

The threats to the continued existence of Aboriginal culture have been, and continue to be, great. Western societies, in particular, accept a linear, progressive notion of history, which they feel justifies their encroachment on less hierarchically developed cultures. European dispossession of Aboriginal lands, the forced transformation of traditional economies, the "education" of Aboriginal children into Western ways, the abolition of traditional spiritual practices and so on, are all justified as doing the work of history (Berger 1991: 25).

Berger's views, represented in his books and in his landmark inquiry, were influenced by the testimony heard during the Mackenzie Valley Pipeline Inquiry from the Dene, who were ambivalent at best about the "progress" that the pipeline project would bring. They had managed to preserve much of their traditional culture and were fearful that development would spell an end to this way of life. Western culture in general, and the Canadian government and business in particular, saw this traditional life as an obstacle to economic growth. Yet the Dene resisted the "lure" of the trappings of modernity, and Berger's analysis was shaped in large part by the resoluteness of their decision. They resisted the characterization of their economy as poor simply because it produced little of cash value, and they did not want to abandon their traditional practices. Berger has been supportive of Aboriginal demands for self-government. He has argued that Canada should recognize the Aboriginal right to self-determination and has urged the state to live by its own laws and treaties. The crux of his argument is that, despite all the threats to Aboriginal culture, its values and beliefs continue to exist and should be allowed to develop freely. They are not in any way inferior, and they deserve to be maintained (Berger 1985: 11). Here Berger is more forceful in his support for the preservation of traditional cultures than NDP policy has been. Subsistence activities can supply the people's needs, provided that these activities are not so curtailed as to make the task impossible. This means that sufficient land and resources must be set aside for use by Aboriginal nations to allow traditional material culture to thrive.

Just as Ryerson and Berger have been influential with the CPC and the NDP respectively, so has George Novack, an American Trotskyist who has written on the Aboriginal question, been influential among the *Communist League/Young Socialists*, the longest-standing and largest of the Trotskyist groups. His short work, *Genocide Against the Indians* (1992), is an answer to the question, "What were the driving forces behind the conflict between the opposing races which inexorably led to its tragic outcome?" (Novack 1992: 4). His answer, in brief, is that the dispossession of Aboriginal lands and the genocide of Aboriginal peoples were outcomes of the conflict between incompatible social and economic forms. The development of a bourgeois society in North America required access to resources such as furs, timber, fish and, above all, land for farming, grazing and settling. Aboriginal peoples were obstacles to this development, and they could not exist alongside the emerging capitalist economy.

> Thus, regardless of their wishes, the Indians and Europeans were sharply counterposed to each other by virtue of their contradictory economic needs and aims. The Indian could maintain his economy with its primitive communistic institutions and customs, its crude division of labor between the sexes and its tribal ties of blood kinship only by keeping the white men at bay. The newcomers could plant their settlements and expand their economic activities only by pressing upon the Indian tribes and snatching their territories. This antagonism, flowing from their diametrically opposing systems of production, governed the dealings between red men and white from their first contacts. (Novack 1992: 11)

Novack argues that there was, and could be, no end to the expansion. The drive to incorporate all of North America into the sphere of capitalist relations had no limit, and so we witness the terrible sufferings and tragedy of peoples being continually moved west through ever-greater degrees of suffering and deprivation (Novack 1992: 15). Critical to Novack's analysis is the argument that the destruction of Aboriginal cultures was inevitable in light of the insatiable appetite of capitalist economies for resources and the greater power of the invaders' form of life.

> I have used the Marxist method of historical materialism to answer this key question. What was involved was the collision of two disparate levels of historical development, two fundamentally different socio-economic formations, two irreconcilable modes of life, types of culture and outlooks upon the world. The defeat of the native tribes was predetermined by the incomparably greater powers of production and destruction, numbers, wealth, and organization, on the side of the classes composing bourgeois civilization. (Novack 1992: 4)

Novack concludes by arguing that the destruction of Aboriginal culture, terrible as it was, could not be avoided. The eventual emergence of a socialist society in America, the development of society according to the stages predicted by Marx, required it.

> The destruction of primitive communism based on common land

> ownership by the Indian tribes was indispensable to the development of American capitalism. The rapid growth of unalloyed bourgeois relations in the United States was made possible by the thoroughness with which the bourgeois forces swept aside all precapitalist institutions, beginning with those of the Indian.
>
> When the American people, under the leadership of the industrial workers, succeed in their task of converting capitalist landed property into public property, they will in effect revive on a far higher level and in more mature forms the common ownership of the soil and the collective use of the means of production that we meet on the very threshold of modern American history.
>
> Thus the struggle for the land in America is reproducing, at its own pace and in its own peculiar ways, the basic pattern of development being traced out by civilized society as a whole. This pattern, too, has been explained and foreseen by the founders of Marxism. (Novack 1992: 24–25)

Novack, like the Trotskyist groups generally, sees Aboriginal economic forms as doomed to extinction. Therefore, the only hope that Aboriginal peoples have for relief from the oppression of capitalism is to join with the revolutionary wing of labour in the effort to replace the current system with socialism. The future for Aboriginal persons is to join the proletariat and its vanguard.

Conclusion

The left groups and intellectuals examined above share a desire to see, in more or less radical form, a transformation in the economic relations presently existing in Canada. The range and type of changes differs markedly from group to group, but all share the view that such change is necessary if the conditions of life for Aboriginal persons are to improve. They all see the racism of Canadian society as a significant obstacle to the enjoyment of full participation in Canadian social and economic life by Aboriginal persons. Socialism, in whatever form, is the hoped-for solution to the problem of racism and the basis for the eventual integration of Aboriginal communities into the culture of the dominant society.

These groups also share a notion of culture that is decidedly non-materialist; they recognize the desire of Aboriginal peoples to preserve their culture and traditions, but they interpret this to mean the preservation of language, values, food and dress and not the continued existence of an economy based on subsistence and sharing. In other words, their vision is that Aboriginal communities will preserve their culture as part of a multicultural mosaic. Those aspects of culture that are personal or are part of a group's social and spiritual practices can be retained. However, little attention is given (with a few exceptions) to the preservation of their traditional material culture. It is taken for granted that the march of history has made traditional economies irrelevant or impossible. Bourgeois society has done its work of universalizing social relations and productive processes, leaving few or no traces of earlier forms of economic life. Therefore, socialism holds out the promise of a more humane incorporation into modernity; one freed from the oppressions of racism. It does not hold out the promise of a return to pre-bourgeois, pre-modern economic practices.

Consequently, there is little support by the left for the national aspirations of Aboriginal communities. The former articulate their interests as an ever-greater technological mastery of nature coupled with an equitable distribution of the wealth produced. The left, especially those groups most influenced by Marx and including the CCF in its early years, sees itself as the inheritor of history, representing the next and higher stage of history. Whether one agrees with the vision of a better society or not, the critical point is that its vision is forward-looking, casting only a passing glance back to the earlier social forms that constitute the guiding ideal for many Aboriginal people.

Part Two

Chapter 3

Aboriginal Apprehensions of Marxism

Marxism and Modernism

The first point that strikes the researcher regarding the responses of Aboriginal groups and intellectuals in Canada to Marxism and the left generally is the paucity of such analysis. Very little has been written on the applicability of Marxism or Marxist thought to the Aboriginal struggle. Whatever one's evaluation of its practical consequences, Marxism's importance in revolutionary and national liberation struggles is beyond doubt. We are forced, therefore, to look to sources outside of Canada for insights into the nature of the response of Aboriginal intellectuals to Marxism.

The central issue raised by those critics who see Marxism as irrelevant at best and incommensurate at worst with traditional Aboriginal culture and future aspirations is Marxism's perceived modernism. Aboriginal critics argue that Marxism is a variant of modernity, that it values technological progress above all else and that it anticipates an almost inevitable passage of society through a pre-ordained system of social formations.

Critics and commentators have long searched for ways to characterize analytically the emergence of the new form of life that, for want of a more descriptive term, is called "modernity." That this concept is often used disparagingly is hardly surprising, as the twentieth century has surpassed all others in the twinned violence of war and economic exploitation. The two world wars in particular gave impetus to analysts who sought to uncover the causes and essential properties of an era that has seemed to shake us loose—or set us free, depending on one's outlook—from the long-familiar pillars that stabilized life. Religion, extended family, place, custom and caste have yielded to consumption, individuality, communication, free thought and social mobility. Science has replaced "myth" just as machines have replaced craft skills. The values and ideas of modernity are seductive. Who would rather have less freedom than more freedom, less consumption than more consumption?

The cultural, social and philosophical project that has come to be known as modernity originated in the critical thought of the Enlightenment. The classical thinkers of this intense and dynamic intellectual period—Rousseau, Voltaire, Diderot and Kant—were, despite their differences, united by a fervent desire to replace the aging Medieval culture by a new, more open one. As philosophers of the emerging bourgeois class, they opposed the political, social and economic privileges of the ancient nobility. They championed rights and freedoms, the removal of restrictions on trade and commercial activity, and the displacement of the overwhelming authority of the Church in matters spiritual and intellectual. In place of religious tradition, they substituted a faith in rational scientific investigation. In place of an oppressive nobility, they argued for republicanism. In place of a static, tradition-bound culture, they looked forward to unending progress. Social and material technologies would, they believed, continue to improve, and humankind could expect that its condition would get progressively better.

Perhaps this belief in progress more than any other characteristic of the Enlightenment project came to represent the new world conceived by these philosophers and ushered in by their revolutionary followers. Modernity and a faith that progress is inevitable became synonymous. The evidence for this article of faith was all around in the subsequent centuries if (and it is surely a big if) one ignored the unimaginable human suffering that progress brought. Factories meant greater production; they also meant sixteen-hour days and child labour. New forms of transportation meant ease of movement; they also meant war on an unimaginable scale. One life could witness changes to a degree that surpassed anything else in history. To give one example, the American philosopher and inheritor of the Enlightenment belief in progress, John Dewey, was born in 1859 in the last days of slavery before the outbreak of the American Civil War. He died in 1952, the year of the first hydrogen bomb test. It would take a whole library simply to list the discoveries and improvements in science and technology that took place during his lifetime. Progress seemed an undeniable fact.

Advancements in technology have now given some societies the capacity to control or transform natural processes beyond even the most optimistic visions of the Enlightenment thinkers. Productive technologies have buried us knee-deep in consumer items while science can image the age and size of the universe itself. Critics of the idea of progress, and of the spiritual and intellectual direction taken by modern societies, have cautioned that the dazzling achievements of modern science and its machines have hidden from us the terrible price to be paid for this progress. Vandana Shiva has studied the ways that the interconnected ideas of progress and development have undermined local and ecologically respectful modes of life and replaced them with the now nearly ubiquitous worship of progress through technology. She understands the imperatives that drive modernity as essentially patriarchal and capitalist. In *Staying Alive* (1988: 5) she wrote:

> [D]evelopment militates against this equality in diversity, and superimposes the ideologically constructed category of western technological man as a uniform measure of the worth of classes, cultures and genders. Dominant modes of perception based on reductionism, duality and linearity are unable to cope with equality in diversity, with forms and activities that are significant and valid, even though different. The reductionist mind superimposes the roles and forms of power of western male-oriented concepts on women, on all non-western peoples and even on nature, rendering all three "deficient," and in need of "development." Diversity, and unity and harmony in diversity, become epistemologically unattainable in the context of maldevelopment, which then becomes synonymous with women's underdevelopment (increasing sexist domination), and nature's depletion (deepening ecological crises). Commodities have grown, but nature has shrunk.

Shiva located the ultimate source of the "maldevelopment" projects, which she sees as destroying local ecologies around the world, in the very philosophical foundation of modernity, in its acceptance of progress through a particular kind of science and technology:

> The basic ontological and epistemological assumptions of reductionism are based on homogeneity. It sees all systems as made up of the same basic constituents, discrete, unrelated and atomistic, and it assumes that all basic processes are mechanical. The mechanistic metaphors of reductionism have socially reconstituted nature and society. In contrast to the organic metaphors, in which concepts of order and power were based on interconnectedness and reciprocity, the metaphor of nature as a machine was based on the assumption of separability and manipulability. (1988: 22)

Related critiques, albeit from very different political perspectives, can be found in the writings of the conservative political philosopher Leo Strauss and the Marxist-influenced analysis of the Frankfurt School. Strauss (1989a, 1989b) has juxtaposed the philosophically based reasonings of the ancients with the more technologically oriented thought of modernity. The former, he has argued, engaged in political philosophizing; they asked questions about the good, about humanity's place in the order of being. Further, they were respectful of the limits of human reasoning. Following Plato, Strauss has argued that our highest achievement is the love of wisdom (that is, philosophy) not wisdom itself. That achievement is the privilege of the gods. In contrast, modernity is in "crisis" because it has replaced meditating on the good with knowledge of the power to make. In his essay "The Three Waves of Modernity" Strauss wrote:

> According to the predominant view, political philosophy is impossible: it was a dream, perhaps a noble dream, but at any rate a dream. While there's broad agreement on this point, opinions differ as to why political philosophy was based on a fundamental error. According to a very widespread view, all knowledge which deserves the name is scientific knowledge; but scientific knowledge cannot validate value judgements; it is limited to factual judgements; yet political philosophy presupposes that value judgements can be rationally validated. (Strauss 1989b: 81–82)

Strauss equated this replacement of philosophy by science with the idea of progress and identified the crisis of modernity as substituting a worship of progress for an adherence to the good (Strauss 1989b: 263–64).

Ironically, similar analyses can be found in the Marxist writings of Max Horkheimer, a founding member of the Frankfurt School and, like Strauss, a German expatriate who fled Naziism. The opening sentences of *Dialectic of Enlightenment* are revealing:

> In the most general sense of progressive thought, the Enlightenment has always aimed at liberating men from fear and establishing their sovereignty. Yet the fully enlightened earth radiates disaster triumphant. The program of the Enlightenment was the disenchantment of the world; the dissolution of myths and the substitution of knowledge for fancy. (Horkheimer and Adorno 1972: 3)

Horkheimer argued that traditional philosophizing which had asked questions about the order of being and the place of human being within this order, had, in the post-Enlightenment period, come to be replaced by what he called "instrumental rationality." Archetypically the form of reasoning employed by the self-interest calculating, economic "man," instrumental rationality is technological in the sense that its sole concern is with the efficient, practical achievement of ends. Reason has become an instrument or tool for accomplishing purposes that are themselves not subject to reasoned analysis and evaluation. This new kind of reasoning is pervasive; it is found in the scientist who creates techniques but is oblivious to social consequences and the businessperson whose goal is profit maximization. The ubiquity of this new kind of formal, technical reasoning has, according to Horkheimer (Horkheimer and Adorno 1972), led modernity to its excesses. The typifying personality of the modern era is Adolf Eichmann, who did his job with spectacular efficiency but who did not seem to grasp the real meaning of his ends, the means to which he executed so "rationally."

For many scholars, especially those influenced by the broad intellectual trend sometimes called "post-modernism," the "modern" political and ideological differences of left–right or Marxist–liberal are relatively unimportant. Rather, they argue that what they share is far more significant than their differences. Both Marxism and liberal capitalism are seen as variants of the Enlightenment project, as representing strains of modernity. Both are thought to accept the capacity of technology to solve problems. Both believe that the good life is intimately tied to increased levels of consumption. Both believe that science is the best, if not the only, road to the truth. Finally, both have faith that human history has been marked by the movement from the worse to the better and that this progress will continue. From the perspective of the post-modern critic, Marxism and capitalism both suffer from all of the deformities of the modern adherence to progress as the *telos* of human social being.

An argument that employs this reading of Marxism can be found in Russell Barsh's article "Contemporary Marxist Theory and Native American Reality" (1988). Barsh states that, despite certain differences, Marxist, and liberal and capitalist thought share a common root.

> Marxism itself [like liberalism] is a logical development from the rise of scientific and technological rationalism at the end of the 18th century. People used science to conquer nature, and Marxism now proposes to use science to overcome the constraints in human society that (in theory) hold back the further progress of conquering nature. (Barsh 1988: 189)

Barsh argues that both movements of modernity—communism and capitalism—"rely on the technological mastery of nature to promise unlimited growth in physical comfort and the elimination of arduous labour" (1988: 189).

However, Barsh's concern is not primarily with an analysis of modernity itself. Rather, he uses the discussion of Marxism as an example of the thinking that typifies modernity and to argue that Marxism is incommensurate with traditional Aboriginal values and understandings and therefore irrelevant to the struggles of Aboriginal communities for justice. Both Marxism and capitalism, at best, can hold out to marginalized Aboriginal persons the prospect of incorporation into an industrialized economy (Barsh 1988: 206–07). Marxists, according to Barsh (1988: 206–07), are willing to address the issues of poverty and unemployment only by promising to proletarianize Aboriginal persons. The deeply ingrained notion in Marxist thought that history moves through certain stages—primitive–communism, ancient–communal, feudal, capitalist and, finally, socialist—inexorably leads Marxists to see so-called "primitive" cultures as doomed to extinction. History is the progressive unfolding of humanity's productive capacities, and so progress demands that the less developed technologically succumb to the more developed. Any "pre-capitalist" Aboriginal culture must give way to more advanced social formations. The best that individual Aboriginal persons can hope for is incorporation into the modern economy without the hindrances of racism and other forms of discrimination.

Barsh argues, therefore, that Marxism has nothing unique to offer Aboriginal communities (1988: 206–07). Its modernness makes it virtually indistinguishable from capitalism. A socialist and a capitalist coalface, for example, are equally alienating and equally antithetical to Aboriginal culture. It is this seemingly inevitable progress of industry, accepted by both the left and the right, which threatens the survival of traditional, non-modern peoples and cultures as well as the planet's ecologies. Any ideology that is committed to the values of modernity is not compatible with the continued existence of traditional life. Barsh concludes:

> In the final analysis, the problem of *industrialism* dwarfs the Left–Right debate as Indian leaders have long maintained. Large-scale technocratic industry concentrates power, alienates workers, unleashes ecological irresponsibility, and increases States' capacity for suicidal warfare without regard to whether production is ultimately controlled by corporate or State bureaucracies. Neither capitalism nor communism offers a proven alternative. One is ethnocidal in effect, and the other by design. It remains to be seen whether the indigenous movement will be able to extricate itself from national contexts and reject the illusion that any industrial ideology is uniquely less spiritual—or more ethnocentric. (Barsh 1988: 208)

That both the left and the right are variants of modernity and accept its basic tenants of progress, technological advancement and so on and that both are destructive of the traditional culture still practised to some degree by

Aboriginal communities are themes echoed by many Aboriginal commentators. Russell Means, a Native American activist and one of the founders of the American Indian Movement (AIM), summarized this view:

> Revolutionary Marxism is committed to even further perpetration and perfection of the very industrial process which is destroying us all. It is offering only to "redistribute" the results, the money maybe, of this industrialization to a wider section of the population.... The only manner in which American Indian people could participate in a Marxist revolution would be to *join* the industrial system, to become factory workers or "proletarians" as Marx called them. The man was very clear that his revolution could only occur through the struggle of the proletariat, that the existence of a massive industrial system is a pre-condition of a successful Marxist society. (1983: 26)

Michael Nofz (1987) took up similar themes in his article comparing Native ideology and Marxism. He argued that the general failure of Marxists to address the issue of Aboriginal peoples and cultures stems from Marxist theory itself; and proposed "that much of what Marx and Engels theorized was more applicable to the modern, industrial tradition and could not be validly transposed to American Indian contexts" (Nofz 1987: 224). He added, "Native American and Euro-Industrial ideologies are therefore not unlike Kuhn's 'incommensurate paradigms.' Beliefs and understandings stemming from either ideological framework will make little sense when apprehended with the assumptions of the other" (Nofz 1987: 227). Nofz then summarized the bases of these conflicting outlooks:

> [Marxist] ideology also encourages a special view of human history. It is inextricably linked to the idea of accumulated progress over the passage of time. Such progress comes with the material transformation of nature and increasingly efficient forms of required technology. Human destiny is assumed to follow a temporal course of increased control over nature. Inventions and discoveries hold significance not only for their present utility, but for their expected contributions to the future acceleration of material production. The past is interpreted in various ways to justify present conditions of human dominance. Less efficient productive activities are not only viewed as evidence for prior "backwardness," or "primitiveness," but also as earlier contributions to current patterns of production and consumption. (1987: 227–28)

In contrast, the thinking of Aboriginal culture is centred around the special relationship that they had to the land as the source of life and survival. As a result, Nofz argues:

> [I]deas of progress marked by the passage of time and increases in production are not given emphasis. The creation of material goods is viewed as a necessary activity, to be sure, but takes on secondary importance to the immediate, sensual experiences with surrounding land. To view natural resources only as materials to be transformed into goods, to see productive activity as the ultimate human goal, would denigrate this affective relationship with land. (1987: 229)

As a consequence of these profound differences in ideational orientation, the two systems of thought are incompatible. Hence Nofz concluded "that the Marxist approach to ideology offers no satisfactory basis for understanding Native American beliefs" (1987: 233).

Important consequences follow from this conclusion. The assumption behind Nofz's argument is that not only do Marxism and traditional cultures differ but that, as a result of these differences, the one cannot intellectually grasp the meaning of the other. If the self-understanding of one culture differs from the conceptual apparatus of another culture, then genuine understanding is impossible. However, in dismissing the relevance of Marxism to the Aboriginal struggle because Marxism and traditional understandings are supposedly incommensurate, Nofz has conflated three distinct and important questions, which are useful to distinguish.

The first is the question of the cross-cultural applicability of methods of social investigation and analysis. Marxism refers to its method of understanding society as "materialism" or "historical materialism." As a method, materialism argues that cultures develop, and hence are properly understood, as emerging from the activities, relationships and thoughts involved in making a living. As Marx said cryptically, "It is just in his work upon the objective world, therefore, that man really proves himself to be a *species-being*. This production is his active species-life" (1977: 74). In other words, cultures in all aspects of this term—economic, political, social and spiritual—are responses to the need to engage oneself in work. Humans are unique among all creatures because how we make our living, how we produce and consume, is subject to thoughtful deliberation and control. We do not simply act on instinct. Cultures are the varying results of the manifold ways that the activities of making our living can be organized. Marx further argued that different cultures have their own conceptual apparatus. People of an industrial, capitalist culture will typically have different understandings of a great variety of issues than people living in a feudal, agriculture society. In a sense, Nofz agrees with this fundamental point. Where he disagrees with the tenets of materialism is in his conclusion that cross-cultural understanding is impossible. He denies that an insight from one culture, namely the materialist argument that ideas and ideologies develop from the organized activities and understandings involved in making a living, can be true for another. If it is consonant with one culture then it cannot be true for another. As an ideology of a modern, industrial culture, therefore, Marxism cannot grasp the meanings of an indigenous culture.

This argument reduces to two possible interpretations. The first is that no theory can, in principle, be applicable to any culture but the one from which it originated. This is Nofz's line of reasoning. The second is that, while cross-cultural dialogue is possible, Marxism in particular is not adequate to the task. The first point is not arguable. Evidence that, for example, Marxist materialism can "explain" the spiritual importance of land in Aboriginal culture by showing that all economic, life-sustaining activities involve an immediate relationship to the land, can be dismissed out of hand. The first interpretation, therefore, is axiomatic in form. It is not the result or conclusion of argument and evidence; rather, it is an assumed starting point for analysis. The second interpretation is more interesting. It is an important task of this book to evaluate if, and how, Marxist thought is relevant to understanding the current situation of Aboriginal communities.

This brings us to the second question. Can Marxism offer practical insight into the relationship between Aboriginal communities and the dominant economic and practical order? Does materialism offer conceptual tools that are valuable in understanding the nature of this relationship and in the struggle to change it? These questions cannot be answered in advance. They are answered over the course of time and through debate and political practice. As we have seen in the previous chapter, the record of the left to date has not been exemplary. Compassion has been co-mingled with veiled contempt.

Finally, the third question concerns the attitude that Marxist thought has towards cultures that are not modern. What place is there in practical struggle, or in analysis, for cultures that utilize less energetic technologies, that is, technologies that have less capacity to produce goods given a fixed labour input? Does Marxism have a place for such cultures in its understanding of historical development?

Aboriginal Critics on Marxism

The responses of a number of Aboriginal writers indicate that the relevance of Marxism to their struggle is limited. An important source of Aboriginal understandings of Marxism is Ward Churchill's *Marxism and Native Ameri-*

cans (1983). Churchill had been struck by the curious silence of the left on Aboriginal issues despite its concern with a variety of other liberation and justice issues. Churchill commissioned leading Aboriginal thinkers in the United States, including Frank Black Elk, Vine Deloria Jr. and Russell Means, to present their analyses of the relevance of Marxism. Four themes emerged again and again in their often scathing evaluation of Marxist thought: 1) Marxism is, in its understanding of issues of relevance to Aboriginal peoples, indistinguishable from its main competitor, capitalism; 2) Marxism accepts the argument that history is the progressive (technological) development of societies through stages from the more primitive to the more developed; 3) as a consequence of this adherence to notions of progress as technological development, Aboriginals and their struggles enter into the range of vision of Marxism only as proletarians and potential participants in the class struggle; and 4) Marxism, like European thought generally, is anti-spiritual and has a fundamentally hostile attitude towards nature.

Theme 1

From the perspective of the contending classes within modern capitalist societies there is a whole world of difference between socialism and capitalism. Tremendous effort has been invested by the bourgeoisie in attacking socialism and demonizing Marx and anyone who follows his teachings. The years immediately following the First World War, the Depression, the 1950s and the Reagan years were all marked by outbursts of anti-Soviet and anti-Marxist fervour. Yet from the perspective of the Aboriginal contributors to Churchill's book, there is little to choose from within the two main twentieth-century political and intellectual alternatives. Frank Black Elk, a Lakota elder, summarized this view:

> A European is a European is a European. Christians, Capitalists, Marxists; all any of them really want from me is my identity as a Lakota, as an "other." All any of them really want of the Lakota is their identity as a people, as something "other" than the understanding (or misunderstanding) of Europe. I, and my people, are just so much more *material* to be accumulated and rearranged into something we weren't and never wanted to be. (1983: 146)

Russell Means was particularly troubled by the issue of uranium mining on the Pine Ridge Reservation in South Dakota. The American government had permitted uranium exploration and mining at Pine Ridge in the 1970s, despite widespread concerns about the effects it would have on health and the environment. Means wrote, "we have a lot of uranium deposits here and white culture (not us) needs this uranium as energy production material" (1983: 24). He asks rhetorically if there would be any difference between a Marxist regime and the present capitalist regime on the issue of mining.

> Look beneath the surface of revolutionary Marxism and what do you find? A commitment to reversing the industrial system which created the need of white society for uranium? No. A commitment to guaranteeing the Lakota and other American Indian peoples real control over the land and resources they have left? No, not unless the industrial process is to be reversed as part of their doctrine. A commitment to our rights, as peoples, to maintaining our values and traditions? No, not as long as they need the uranium within our land to feed the industrial system of the society, the culture of which the Marxists *are still a part*. (Means 1983: 25)

On this issue Marxism and capitalism share their commitment to industrial development as the exemplar of progress; and so, from the standpoint of the Lakota, who are trying to prevent the devastation likely to be caused by continued mining, both ideological variants appear to be the same.

Theme 2

A common reading of Marx, and one that is echoed in the writings of Aboriginal critics, is the notion that Marxism is a theory of the development—often thought as inevitable—of human societies through successive stages. Marx and Engels wrote in the *German Ideology* (1966) that human culture has passed through a discrete number of stages, each developing from the one before it. In the beginning was primitive-communism. This long period, which includes most Aboriginal peoples of Turtle Island, was marked by communally held property, relative equality between the sexes and an absence of coercive state mechanisms. This period was followed by the first class-divided society, the state-communal, which was typical of ancient Greece and Rome. This evolved into feudalism which gave way to capitalism. Socialism is theorized as the inevitable outcome of a number of contradictions inherent in the capitalist system, particularly the clash between the "property-less" proletarians and the property-owning bourgeoisie.

The difficulty that this historical periodization has for defenders of Aboriginal culture is that it appears, on the surface at least, to have branded traditional culture as a historically transcended phase. If such cultures continue to exist it is only because they have not yet been developed technologically, socially and politically. They are backward societies whose destiny is to be modernized. George Tinker wrote:

> [If] Marxist thinking and the notion of a historical dialectic were finally proven correct, then American Indian people and all indigenous peoples would be doomed. Our cultures and value systems, our spirituality, and even our social structures, would give way to an emergent socialist structure that would impose a notion of the good on all people regardless of ethnicity and culture. (Tinker 1992: 15–16)

In other words, history evolves according to dialectical laws—the laws of the necessary movement of culture and thought. One can optimistically describe this progress through stages as a positive development, or one can lament the passing of noble forms of life that are worthy of our respect. In the end, though, neither attitude matters. Historical laws unfold with an unyielding force, and those whom history has passed by cannot survive. On this reading, Marx is very close to Hegel (1956: 63–64) who argued that societies that no longer embody the progressive movement of history are doomed to extinction or, at the very least, the status of ignored backwater.

Ward Churchill drew upon such notions of progress and inevitable historical trajectories when he wrote:

> From first to last, Marxists insist upon the specific inevitability of industrialization and capitalism as sanctification of their "science" in the same fashion that biologists approach theirs: through assertion of unassailable physical *fact*. From this perspective, Marxists can no more step outside their preconceptions of order to seriously entertain other considerations than a responsible biologist could reasonably engage in professional discourse on the aeronautical characteristics of the blue whale. (1983: 187)

The specific form that the notion of historical progress through stages from lower to higher takes regarding Aboriginal culture is based on the assumed superiority of those societies that employ technologies more intensively.

> First, it seems Marxists are hung up on exactly the same ideas of "progress" and "development" that are the guiding motives of those they seek to overthrow. They have this idea that Lakotas are (or, at least, were) a primitive people in relation to Europe. Any rational person would have to ask what's so "primitive" about a people which managed to maintain a perpetually democratic way of life, which shared all social power equitably between both sexes and various age groups, which considered war essentially a sport rather than an excuse to indulge in the wanton slaughter of masses

> of people, which killed game only for food rather than as a "sport," which managed to occupy its environment for thousands and thousands of years without substantially altering it (that is to say, destroying it). That same rational person would have to ask why any sane individual would not choose to live that way if the chance were available, or aspire towards such an existence if the chance wasn't immediate. (Churchill 1983: 141–42)

Theme 3

Related to the idea of human progress as marked by the intensification of the use of technology is the alienation from the natural world commonly experienced by Western society. Vine Deloria Jr. (1983) argues that Western culture is separated from and exploitative of the environment precisely because of the technologies and "progress" that it celebrates. The machineries of production allow us to operate on the natural world at a distance, and they have given us the power to remake nature. Guided by our own sense of technological possibility and the ideal of efficiency, we have alienated ourselves from the real source of our existence. As a consequence, Western thinkers and religious figures have emphasized the need for salvation through an overcoming of this alienation (Deloria 1983: 114–16). Deloria sees Marxism, in particular, as a variant of this primordial urge to transcend the transcendence of the natural:

> The implications of Marxist thinking may be revolutionary for Western peoples but they raise a strange response in American Indians. Why is it that Western peoples feel themselves alienated from nature? And why is it that they seek some kind of messianic, ultra-historical solution once they have identified this estrangement? To consider communism, even in its purest form, the *definitive* resolution between humanity and nature is basically to announce that the alienation of humanity and nature is the fundamental problem around which all others revolve. Since this problem is so continuously on the minds of Western peoples, and since, after all the economic analyses are concluded, Marx returns to this theme, a better use of one's time than advocacy of capitalism or communism might be an examination of how Western peoples decided or when they first experienced this alienation—since it does not occur within the American Indian context as a problem of this magnitude. Marxism would therefore appear to be simply another Christian denomination, albeit a highly secularized version, seeking to discover the Messiah and opposing the "Kingdom of this world." (Deloria 1983: 131–32)

Therefore Marxism is at best useless to Aboriginal peoples. The struggle of the latter is not to overcome the separation from nature, as it is for Western thought. Rather, Aboriginal culture in its traditional forms still retains the integrity of the human–natural relationship. Its struggle is to preserve a culture that has not yet experienced the disruption from the natural. Furthermore, the actual form that the reconciliation with the natural takes in Western thought (including Marxist thought) is inimical to Aboriginal life. The gulf between human existence and nature is to be overcome by making the natural more human and reasonable; that is, the alienation that Western culture experiences is to be transcended through a re-working of the natural into a form commensurate with human desire and being. In Aboriginal thought the harmony that exists between the human and the natural does so because humans adapt themselves to the patterns and rhythms of nature (Deloria 1983: 124–26).

Theme 4

The consequence of the above three points for political practice is that, according to Russell Means (1983), Marxists are interested only in the liberation of people as proletarians, that is, as workers in an industrialized economy. This implies that all revolutionary activity, all action designed to liberate the masses from oppression, must be oriented towards the interests of the proletariat:

> The only manner in which American Indian people could participate in a Marxist revolution would be to *join* the industrial system, to become factory workers or "proletarians" as Marx called them. The man was very clear about the fact that his revolution could occur only through the struggle of the proletariat, that the existence of a massive industrial system is a precondition of a successful Marxist society. (Means 1983: 26)

To date, there has not been much support for the Aboriginal struggle by organized labour anywhere in North America. Therefore, to tie their struggle to the prior struggle of the proletariat will likely force Aboriginal people to abandon that which makes them unique—the desire for the survival of what Marxists call a "pre-capitalist" culture.

The post-contact history of Aboriginal peoples, as well as the attitudes and analyses of the left in the past sixty years, makes their rejection of Marxism understandable, if lamentable. The history of the relationship between Aboriginal societies and European "immigrants" or "invaders" has been one in which the latter have tried to obliterate, physically and culturally, the former. When the attempted destruction of the people came to an end, the destruction of the culture continued. Aboriginal resistance, as we saw in Chapter One, took the form of preserving their culture, of steadfastly struggling against assimilation. Of course, the effects of 500 years of colonization have been great. While much of the tradition has survived, much also has been lost. What remains, however, is a self-conscious identity as Aboriginal and a desire to resist further assimilation. To identify oneself as Indian or Aboriginal means placing oneself inside a twinned tradition. First, there is for each society and culture a group of practices, a language, understandings, historical memories and so on. Second, there is the shared experience of colonialism and resistance. In some important measure Aboriginal identity in this century involves a commitment to preserving the traditional culture. No "liberation" movement that fails to be mindful and respectful of this identity can resonate with contemporary Aboriginal struggles or be meaningful to Aboriginal peoples. The critiques of Marxism by Ward Churchill, Vine Deloria Jr., Russell Means, Frank Black Elk and others are informed by the sense that, as a Western political, economic and philosophic system, Marxism emanates from the same cultural values that are trying to destroy what is Aboriginal. Industrialism, technology, consumerism, alienation from and control over nature are destroying what is Aboriginal as surely as are land grabs and extermination policies. One may be better intentioned, but the consequences are thought to be the same. It remains to be seen whether the reading of Marxism that underlies their criticisms is correct. However, they are reacting to real strains within left thinking on Aboriginal "issues."

Dissenting Voices

By no means is there absolute unanimity among Aboriginal critics regarding the relevance of Marxist or left thinking. There are a few authors who are critical of the rejection of the relevance of left analysis and wish to reappraise the potential of Marxist-inspired analysis for understanding the current relationship between Aboriginal societies and the wider society. Gary Anders, a member of the Cherokee nation, and Howard Adams, a leading Métis spokesperson, have used the analyses of colonialism in making sense of their current situation.

Gary Anders (1980) has studied the causes of the economic underdevelopment and poverty of Cherokee communities in the United States. After testing a variety of hypotheses, Anders concluded that the theoretical model that best fits the experience of Cherokee communities is that found in dependency literature. Originally developed to explain underdevelopment in Latin America, dependency theory postulates that the "historical process of colonialism" operates by the establishment within the colonized people of a local ruling elite. This indigenous elite, or "comprador" class, acts as agents of the dominant or colonizing power. Rather than ruling directly by a system of colonial administration, the European and North American colonial powers established local ruling classes. These classes controlled the indigenous society and insured the continued extraction of surplus value and resources for the colonizing power, in return for which their dominance was supported and their loyalty rewarded. The local society remains underdeveloped because any surpluses it generates, any resources it has, are siphoned off to the colonizing power by the comprador class. Tribal elites among the Cherokee, Anders argued, were set up by the American government to facilitate such resource transfers:

> On the basis of my research with the Oklahoma Cherokees, I found that colonial relations between whites and Indians effected a reorganization of the tribe's social institutions and resulted in the creation of an internal *comprador* class which was used repeatedly by the government to authorize unconscionable land sales. Through this process, traditional tribal structures were undermined and adapted to fit white needs. The net result was a gradual constriction of Indian sovereignty and initiative. (Anders 1980: 693)

The effects that the comprador class has on the development of Cherokee society and economy have been devastating:

> These *compradors* perpetuate the Cherokees' underdevelopment by using the tribe's resources to promote the interests of the dominant white economy at the expense of the tribe. The Oklahoma Cherokees remain underdeveloped despite massive injections of federal funds because their tribal economy is entirely controlled by a powerful class of "white Indians." In fact, this small ruling elite has been able to gain effective control over the tribe's resource base. It has transformed the once self-sufficient Cherokee tribal economy into one completely oriented toward using Indian poverty as a means of securing lucrative government antipoverty grants that eventually wind up in the hands of the local white contractors, merchants, and businessmen. (Anders 1980: 694)

Howard Adams, a Métis from Saskatchewan, is a retired professor of Native Studies who has written a number of books analyzing the politics and economic life of Métis communities. Although their legal status differs from that of status Indians, Métis, especially those who live in the Métis colonies on the Prairies, have experienced many of the same relationships with the Canadian state and the contemporary economy that status Indians have (Adams 1984, 1995). As such, his analysis is of relevance to a general study of Aboriginal–Canadian relations. Like Anders, Adams uses the concept of colonialism that has been developed in the extensive literature on development, modernization and national liberation struggles in the Third World. The mechanics of colonial rule, which Adams describes, closely resemble those discussed by Anders.

> Colonizers are still using the old system of "divide and rule." Immediately comes to mind the conflict in South Africa between Mandela's ANC and the Zulus; as well as the war between the Tamils and Hindus in Sri Lanka and tribal civil wars in Rwanda and Somalia—to name a few. Most Third World nations are ruled by military dictatorships of co-opted Native leaders who are manipulated by an imperial nation, usually the United States. (Adams 1995: 10)

Important consequences for the current political debates follow from this conceptual framework. As we have seen, the form that the need for autonomy and cultural survival has taken in the face of overwhelming pressures to assimilate has frequently been the demand for self-government. This idea, that Aboriginal communities must regain a measure of sovereignty and governance over their own affairs, became the focus of the political efforts to preserve traditional culture, particularly after the release of the White Paper in 1969. By the 1980s there developed among Aboriginal leaders, especially the chiefs elected under the *Indian Act*, a rough consensus, in principle at least, that self-government should be the goal of federal policy. Of course, there were, and are, important differences of opinion as to what the idea means, what will be the extent of powers exercised by Aboriginal communities and what will be the actual entity exercising self-government (a reserve, a band, a nation). Adams' (1995) dependency model of the evolution of Métis colonies (and one could easily add, reserve communities) indicates that caution must be exercised before self-government arrangements can be concluded. In particular, careful study of the communities themselves reveals the profound and damaging effects of decades of colonial rule (Adams 1995). A comprador class has emerged and their interests are at odds with the mass of the people:

> As the mass of underclass Natives, we need to mobilize as a political force to stop the collaboration and exploitation by such comprador rule. The move for so-called self-government can be a dangerously oppressive and reactionary move.
>
> The consciousness and behaviour of Native collaborator lead-

> ers have sharpened since the rise of neocolonialism. They do not only identify with the oppressor, they have actually become the new Aboriginal oppressors. With the support of governments and multinational corporations, they have become much more brutal and vicious than white imperial rulers. (Adams 1995: 10–11)

Integral to the struggle for liberation from the effects of colonial domination is the need to tell the truth about colonialism. As Adams notes, mystifications about the history of Canada and about the evolution of Métis society itself serve only to reinforce the oppression that is part of everyday life for the Métis and other Aboriginal peoples in Canada:

> The essays examine how eurocentric historical interpretation of Indians, Métis and Inuit are used to justify conquest and to camouflage government mechanisms in maintaining oppression. The authentic history of Indians and Métis has been hidden or falsified by establishment academics who use distortions and stereotypes to obscure the harsh political and colonial practices of the state.
>
> After five hundred years of colonial oppression, Indians, Métis and Inuit have internalized a colonized consciousness. The colonizer's falsified stories have become universal truths to mainstream society, and have reduced Aboriginal culture to a caricature. This distorted reality is one of the most powerful shackles subjugating Aboriginal people. It distorts all indigenous experiences, past and present, and blocks the road to self-determination.
>
> Honesty for Indian and Métis history and culture is more than a quest for decolonization and national identity; it is a pursuit to transform imperial structures of the state. History, as told by authentic Aboriginal historians, does more than retell establishment history. It explains the struggles for self-determination and promotes efforts to overcome present colonization. Indian and Métis liberation is not possible if eurocentricism is not terminated. (1995: 1)

Adams is especially critical of Ward Churchill and the other contributors to the volume *Marxism and Native Americans* (1983). Marxist thought in particular and left analysis in general offer important opportunities for understanding the causes of and solutions to the oppression of Aboriginal peoples in North America. Adams argues that this opportunity was lost because Churchill did not take seriously the positive contributions that Marxist analysis can make (1984: 58). Instead, he dismissed it out of hand because it shares the same lineage as the capitalist system, which is actually exploiting Aboriginal people (Adams 1984: 59). The authors "had an exceptional opportunity to study an important issue" but they did not rise above the stereotyping of Marxist thought (Adams 1984: 58).

Roland Christjohn (1998), a psychologist and educational consultant for Alberta First Nations, and a Cree, has spoken of the difficulties he has encountered when introducing Marxism into discussions of the future of Aboriginal–state relations both nationally and in Alberta. Undoubtedly, this was due in part to the heating up of the Cold War under the Reagan and Bush administrations and to the consequent disillusionment felt by many about the usefulness of Marxism after the fall of the Soviet Union. The past two decades have seen a growing rejection of things modern. Science is attacked; medicine is questioned; reason itself is challenged as the source of truth. This scepticism is coupled with a surprising faith in the mystical and unknown. Belief in angels outstrips belief in evolution in the United States. Marxism is attacked or ignored because it is seen as part of the project of the Enlightenment, which sought to gain control over the natural and social environment.

When we examine the analyses and evaluations of Marxism we see that those who are critical of Marxism locate the cause of the oppression of Aboriginal cultures in North America in the intellectual and philosophical underpinnings of Western, modern life. In other words, Barsh, Nofz, Deloria, Black Elk, Tinker, Churchill and Means see the source of dispossession, exploitation and assimilation in the ideological structures of Western society. While Marxism is not hegemonic, it is part of that general form of thought and is, therefore, rejected. Anders and Adams, on the other hand, locate the source of oppression in the specific economic and political relationships that are integral to the capitalist system. Specifically, they agree that a colonialist relationship exists, such that Aboriginal communities are dominated by local elites who act in the interests of the political and economic elites, who in turn dominate the larger society. Hence, as a philosophy that challenges the domination of the bourgeoisie and the political relationships of bourgeois society, Marxism is analytically useful and its followers are potential political allies.

CHAPTER 4

MARXISM AND THE ABORIGINAL QUESTION

THE TRAGIC SENSE

In the previous chapter we saw that some Aboriginal thinkers have reacted to a reading of Marx and Marxism which they see as inimical to the struggle of Aboriginal peoples for the survival of a traditional culture. Marxism was condemned as a variant of modernity, which, like capitalism, stresses the inevitability and value of technological progress. In this chapter we examine Marx's own views on the question of Aboriginal culture. We also explore the particular readings or interpretations of Marx underlying the left's analysis, arguing that this reading is one-sided. Furthermore, we present an alternative reading of Marx, one which we believe is truer to Marx's own analysis and more compatible with the practical goals of the contemporary Aboriginal movement.

The writings of Marx and Engels on pre-capitalist societies, that is, those social formations that pre-date capitalism, including slave societies, feudalism and so on, cover a wide range of topics and appear in a number of their works. They also draw upon a variety of sources, most important being the writings of Lewis Henry Morgan (1818–1881), an American anthropologist who specialized in the study of the Iroquois. Morgan's most notable works are *League of the Iroquois* (1962) and *Ancient Society* (1964). The former details the culture of the Iroquois, with special attention to clans as the basis of the social organization underlying the confederacy. The latter text presented a more general analysis of the stages of the evolution of "primitive" societies.

Morgan's influence on Marx and Engels was substantial. According to Marx, Morgan's *Ancient Society* inaugurated a revolution in the study of early societies that rivaled Darwin's impact on the study of biological evolution. Engels titled his own work *The Origin of the Family, Private Property and the State in the Light of the Researches of Lewis H. Morgan* (1884) recognizing this debt to Morgan. Engels' text begins: "Morgan was the first person with expert knowledge to attempt to introduce a definite order into the prehistory of man"; it ends with a long quotation from *Ancient Society,* in which Morgan looks forward to the day when society will evolve beyond the need for private property and return to the "liberty, equality and fraternity of the ancient gentes."

Engels (1979) wrote to Karl Kautsky (February 16, 1884) of the debt he and Marx owed to Morgan. Marx had made extensive notes on Morgan's *Ancient Society*, intending perhaps to write on the subject of primitive society; and Engels wrote *The Origin* as a posthumous completion of Marx's project. In the preface to the 1884 edition Engels states, "My work can offer but a meagre substitute for that which my departed friend was not destined to accomplish. However, I have before me, in his extensive extracts from Morgan, critical notes which I reproduce here whenever this is at all possible" (1983: 5). Marx's extensive commentary on *Ancient Society* has been reproduced in *The Ethnological Notebooks of Karl Marx* (Krader 1974); the commentary on Morgan covers 147 pages, including thirty pages on the Iroquois Confederacy.

Engels summarizes Morgan's contribution to Marxist thought in the preface to the 1891 edition (17–18). First is Morgan's discovery of the descent of gens (or clan) membership from the mother and the practice of exogamy based on the gens. Second is the so-called mother-right; among the Iroquois, a form of social organization existed that pre-dated patriarchy and involved a much higher status for women than later "father-right" cultures. The question of "mother-right" and its prevalence among traditional societies is now questioned (Fluehr-Lobban 1979). Engels, however, accepted it; and the existence of ancient societies, particularly the Iroquois, among whom women were relatively equal to men became the starting point for Engels' anthropological writings.

The critical concept of Engels' (and Marx's) anthropology is the notion that traditional or "primitive" societies differed significantly from all later social forms. Designating these traditional formations as primitive communism, Marx and Engels argue, on the basis of Morgan's research, that these cultures had relative equality between men and women, no private property, no classes and hence no class conflict and no state in the sense of an organized system of coercion and enforced relations. These four characteristics of primitive communism were typical of most or all human prehistory. The descriptions that Marx and Engels offered of such societies were overlaid with a mixture of nostalgia and lament. Their sense of the history of human kind was tragic. On the one hand, these societies represent what is good and humane in all social organizations. They were uncorrupted and cooperative. They exhibited the truth of Rousseau's saying "Man is born free." There were no slaves and no masters, no serfs and no kings. No one could be coerced to act, and family life was marked by equality and reciprocity. On the other hand, their level of productivity, of the use of the technologies of production, made them unable to resist the invasions from European states or to develop the "high" culture of Western societies (Engels 1983: 98). The following quotation captures Engels' sense of the sad but inevitable replacement of these traditional societies by modern, progressive social forms:

> And this gentile constitution is wonderful in all its childlike simplicity! Everything runs smoothly without soldiers, gendarmes or police; without nobles, kings, governors, prefects or judges; without prisons; without trials.... Those concerned decide, and in most cases century-old custom has already regulated everything. There can be no poor and needy—the communistic household and the gens know their obligations towards the aged, the sick and those disabled in war. All are free and equal—including the women. There is as yet no room for slaves, nor, as a rule, for the subjugation of alien tribes. When the Iroquois conquered the Eries and the "Neutral nations" about the year 1651, they invited them to join the Confederacy as equal members.... Let us not forget, however, that this organization was doomed to extinction. It never developed beyond the tribe.... The gentile constitution in full bloom, as we have seen it in America, presupposed an extremely undeveloped form of production, that is, an extremely sparse population spread over a wide territory, and therefore the almost complete domination of man by external nature, alien, opposed, incomprehensible to him, a domination reflected in his childish religious ideas. (1983: 96–98)

Marx also articulates the sense of loss inevitably intermingled with all progress. Progress is tragic in the sense that, like the tragedy of ancient Greece, our fate can be transcended only if we either are extremely fortunate or expend great effort.

Marx is enormously indebted to the German philosopher G.W.F. Hegel for his understanding of history. Marx draws from Hegel the idea that history unfolds dialectically, through a series of stages that follow one another. For Marx, the original, idyllic, pre-historic unity is not the sense of being at home in one's culture, as it is for Hegel. Rather, it is the unity of production and consumption, of thought and action, of design and execution, which is typical of labouring in societies without private property or wage labour. For Hegel, the originally unified experience of early cultures was fractured, leaving humanity unsettled socially, politically and philosophically. In early Greek society the individual person took the whole culture of his or her *polis* to be their own identity. There was no individualism in the modern sense. History and philosophy commence when this unity is sundered, when people begin to question the values of their culture and to substitute their own judgements and opinions for those of their society. This subjectivity is both the beginning of free thought and the precondition for the achievement of philosophical truth and scientific understanding. It is also, however, unsettling. It leaves us adrift, without boundaries or limits to thought or behaviour, without any moorings or maps. History is the striving to reunite ourselves and our individuality with the truth and ideas of our society, that is, to see and feel our culture as our own identity. The "progress" towards this recapturing of a unity in life and experience is painful. Even in the achievement of the quest for unity, humanity yearns for the simplicity of its youth. Now, when we have reacquired this unity through science and philosophy, we are aware that the relationship between our own personal being and our community, the sense that we are integrally tied to a larger whole, is primarily conceptual. It is thought rather than felt, and we long still for the immediate feeling of identity that has been lost.

Marx takes this outline of human history and reinterprets the content of the categories. The original unity of experience is not the immediate identity of a culture as one's own but rather the unity of the labouring activity. The pre-historical individual was not alienated or separated in any way from the natural materials of production, the decisions regarding what or how to produce or the productive process itself. As a result, these early communistic societies were free from alienation and hence free from the antagonistic social relations that result from alienated production. The gradual introduction of private property meant that labour became alienated. Someone other than the labourer her/himself controlled the resources and means of production and determined the what and how of production. For Marx, this original fall marked the beginning of history, and history's course is the movement or "progress" towards finally overcoming the separation of the person from their labour in communism. Like Hegel, Marx sometimes argues that the general sweep of history was inevitable. However, this development has a tragic dimension. Human societies that had no private property had no alienation. Each person worked directly with nature, and there was no place for relations of hierarchy or domination.

> Thus the ancient conception, in which man always appears (in however narrowly national, religious or political a definition) as the aim of production, seems very much more exalted than the modern world, in which production is the aim of man and wealth the aim of production. In fact, however, when the narrow bourgeois form has been peeled away, what is wealth, if not the universality of needs, capacities, enjoyments, productive powers, etc. of individuals, produced in universal exchange?... What is this, if not a situation where man does not reproduce himself in any determined form, but produces his totality? Where he does not seek to remain something formed by the past, but is in the absolute movement of becoming? In bourgeois political economy—and in the epoch of production to which it corresponds—this complete elaboration of what lies within man, appears as the total alienation, and the destruction of all fixed, one-sided purposes, as the sacrifice of the end in itself to a wholly external compulsion. Hence in one way the childlike world of the ancients appears to be superior; and this is so, in so far as we seek for closed shape, form and established limitation. The ancients provide a narrow satisfaction, whereas the modern world leaves us unsatisfied, or, where it appears to be satisfied with itself, is *vulgar* and *mean*. (Marx 1965: 84–85)

Marx articulated the double sense of progress as "progressive," that is, as the movement towards the eventual overcoming of the alienation of labour, and as tragic, that is, that this movement involves the destruction of local, traditional social forms, in his 1853 articles "The British Rule in India" and "The Future Results of British Rule in India." These articles include all of the contradictory and conflicting tendencies of his analysis. Both were written for the *New York Daily Tribune,* for which Marx was an occasional correspondent. In the first article, "The British Rule in India," Marx argues that, whereas previous invasions of India changed only the superficial political arrangements leaving village life untouched, the British invasion has destroyed the entire framework of life. The British introduced capitalist relations into India, putting the village weaver in India into competition with the Birmingham factory labourer. As a result, traditional life was destroyed (Marx 1968a: 84–85). In the second article, Marx writes: "England has to fulfill a double mission in India: one destructive, the other regenerating—the annihilation of old Asiatic society, and the laying of the material foundations of Western society in Asia" (1968b: 125).

Later in the second article Marx wrote that capitalism is the dynamic economic system of the modern world, one that powerfully tends towards universalization. It spreads across the whole world, transforming all other types of economies and cultures into its own image. It is a progressive force, destroying all that is before it and creating a world market (1968b: 130). Marx states that the "bourgeois period of history has to create the material basis of the new world," specifically "universal intercourse" and the continued "development of the productive forces" (1968b: 131). The consequences of this progress are horrifying for traditional peoples:

> [When] a great social revolution shall have mastered the results of the bourgeois epoch, the market of the world and the modern powers of production, and subjugated them to the common control of the most advanced peoples, then only will human progress cease to resemble that hideous pagan idol who would not drink the nectar but from the skulls of the slain. (Marx 1968b: 131)

This social transformation cannot come from the resistance struggles of the indigenous peoples. Marx asserts:

> Indians will not reap the fruits of the new elements of society scattered among them by the British bourgeoisie, till in Great Britain itself the now ruling classes shall have been supplanted by the industrial proletariat, or till the Hindoos themselves shall have grown strong enough to throw off the English yoke. (1968b: 127–28)

Until they have left their traditional culture behind they cannot successfully resist capitalism. Therein lies the tragic irony. Traditional peoples must embrace modernity to resist it.

How do we account for this tragic sense in the writings of Marx and Engels? The answer is found in a certain ambivalence in their thought. On one hand, capitalism is progressive because it creates the conditions for the emergence of socialism and eventually communism. It does this, in part, by dramatically increasing the productive capacity of society. On the other hand, capitalism's spread, and the intensification of technologies of production co-terminus with this advance, immeasurably increase the alienation that those from traditional cultures experience. Marx's writings are infused with tension between the final good and the terrible suffering needed to bring it about.

In part, as well, there is an ambiguity in Marx's thought regarding the issue of whether, in the final analysis, it is advancements in technology or the class struggle that is the determining factor in historical development. As we will see, some commentators argue that changes in the technologies of production bring about changes in all other aspects of life. In other words, one set of technologies—the hand-loom is the most frequently cited example—gave us the feudal period, while the steam powered loom resulted in capitalism. Others argue that the core of Marxism is the claim that history is the story of the class struggle, that the result of class conflict drives history. If one argues the former then the likelihood is that the spread of capitalist social relations will be seen as inevitable and largely positive. Accentuating class struggle, though, can result in a different evaluation; one is less inclined to support the spread of capitalism when it is seen as a struggle between a capitalist class and a local indigenous population. Marx himself would reject such "either/or" readings often found in commentaries. However, our purpose here is to elucidate where certain readings originate theoretically and their consequences for political practice.

The National Question

The national question, that is, the rise of nationalism and nationalist movements and the issue of the right of national self-determination, has become increasingly important in Marxist circles in the past decades. It is useful to examine this issue for a number of reasons. First, it helps illuminate important theoretical questions in the analysis of Marx's thought. Second, Aboriginal nationalism and the demand for self-government, as well as more radical demands for independence require a response by the left.

Shlomo Avineri (1990) provides an interesting analysis of the ambiguity of Marx's position on the national question and related theoretical issues. Arguing that "Marx never discussed nationalism in any systematic way," Avineri nonetheless identifies two often conflicting paradigms or "distinct analyses":

> The *locus classicus* for the premodern paradigm [in Marx's pre-1848 writings] (Paradigm I) is to be found in the *Communist Manifesto*, where the universalizing power of the capitalist market is sketched by Marx in memorable and pithy language. This universalizing thrust, according to Marx, does away with everything that is particular, be it regional or national.... National differences thus are likened in this paradigm to other premodern traits, like local customs and dress: they are all due to disappear before the universalizing onslaught of the bourgeoisie and be even more perfectly integrated into a world-culture by the proletarian revolution. (1990: 447)

Marx here emphasized the creation of a common culture in which prejudices based on religion, language, ethnicity and so on would be submerged into a universal world culture based on the shared experiences of a world capitalist, and later socialist, economy.

Impressed by continuing and powerful nationalisms that did much to block the revolutions of 1848, Marx reformulated his position on the national question (Avineri 1990: 448). Paradigm II, developed in Marx's post-1848 writings, explained nationalism

> as a modern superstructural expression of the bourgeois need for larger markets and territorial consolidation. In this paradigm, far from being an exotic and romantic, or romanticized, relic of the pre-industrial age, nationalism becomes (to use Eric Hobsbawm's later phrase) a "building block" of capitalism. (Avineri 1990: 448)

This second understanding saw some nationalist movements as critical to the development of capitalism in Europe and worldwide. So, for example, after 1848 Marx no longer interpreted German unification as a pre-modern and largely irrational urge for Germanness but rather as critical to the economic development of Germany as a whole. Such a progress towards full articulation of capitalist relations serves only to hasten the emergence of a world capitalist economy and its inevitable replacement by socialism. Similarly, Marx criticized and opposed nationalist movements in the Austro-Hungarian Empire, for example, by Czechs and Croatians. These secessionist movements would in no way help the maturing of economic relations in these countries or in Eastern Europe generally. They were reactionary "in the sense that should they succeed, industrial and economic development in Central and Eastern Europe [would] … be slowed down, and hence the eventual victory of the proletariat [would] … be hampered" (Avineri 1990: 448).

Interestingly, in both paradigms identified by Avineri, Marx is ultimately committed to whatever advances the development of capitalist relations. Common to both paradigms is the belief that what should determine the left's attitude towards national movements is whether or not they contribute towards the maturing of capitalism. While Marx changed his mind on key issues relating to German nationalism after 1848, Avineri argues that he did so because he came to see German nationalism not as a hindrance but as critical to the progress of capitalism. Nationalist sentiments themselves were given no value by Marx; nationalist movements were good if they were thought to move history forward (and develop capitalism) and bad if they retarded its progress. This commitment never changed (Avineri 1990).

Ephraim Nimni (1989: 297) argues that there is a unity in Marx's and Engels' various positions on the national question:

> The main parameters of this paradigm are derived from three conceptions widely considered central to historical materialism: the theory of evolution; the theory of economic determination of the forces of production; and a derivative category of both, the Eurocentric bias in the analysis of concrete case studies.

The first conception, the theory of evolution, "holds that social transformation can be grasped in universal laws of historical development" (Nimni 1989: 297), that is, history moves through a series of discrete, necessary stages from the earliest, primitive communism to the most advanced socialism. The second conception, economic reductionism, "declares that all meaningful changes within the social arena take place in the sphere of economic (class) relations" (Nimni 1989: 297). Political forms, ideologies and philosophical ideas are all reducible to and dependent upon the specific economic formation of the time. The third parameter, Eurocentric bias, "refers to the construction of a model of development which universalizes empirically observed European categories of development" (Nimni 1989: 298). Nimni argues that the first two conceptions are European-derived. They may be true in general for a certain time and place, such as nineteenth-century Europe, but they are not universally true (Nimni 1989: 298).

Nimni claims that, as a result of these three underlying conceptions, Marx developed a position on the national question appropriate only to certain specific societies, for example France in the period after the Revolution. Nimni articulates a reading of Marx on the national question which is similar to Avineri's Paradigm II:

> In this context the different treatment given by Marx and Engels to different national communities acquires meaning and coherence. The "modern nation" is an epiphenomenal result of the development of the bourgeoisie as the hegemonic class, and the former must be evaluated on the merits of the latter. If it represents a higher stage of development of the productive forces in relation to a pre-determined process of historical change; if it abolishes the feudal system by building a "national state," then the nationalist movement deserves support as a "tool" for progressive social change. If, however, the nationalist movement emerges among linguistic or cultural communities incapable of surviving the upheavals of capitalist transformation, because they are too small or have a weak or non-existent bourgeoisie, then the nationalist movement becomes a "regressive" force—one which is incapable of overcoming the stage of "peasant–feudal" social organization.

> Marx and Engels repeatedly argued that national communities incapable of constituting "proper national states" should "vanish" by being assimilated into more "progressive" and "vital" nations. (Nimni 1989: 304)

This distinction between progressive and retrograde national communities is based on the three conceptions outlined above and is the key to understanding why Marx supported the Irish nationalist desire for independence from Britain but opposed nationalist movements among the "South Slavs." The nationalist movements of communities that cannot form the political basis for a national bourgeoisie are reactionary and should not be supported by the left. They will never develop the local bourgeoisie, which is the first precondition for proletarian revolution, and so their national aspirations are pre-modern and reactionary. Nimni concludes that, for Marx,

> these usually small national communities are not only "functionally" reactionary, but *intrinsically* reactionary relics of the past, which must disappear to pave the way for social progress. Since the only purpose of national agitation is the drive to build a national state, national communities that because of their size are not viable independent economic units have no *"raison d' être."* (1989: 309)

The interpretation of Ephraim Nimni, and by extension of Shlomo Avineri, has not gone unchallenged. Enzo Traverso and Michael Löwy as well as John Hoffman and Nxumalo Mzala have questioned not only Nimni's reading of Marx on the national question but the veracity of his attempt to underpin this reading with what he takes to be the core ideas of historical materialism. Traverso and Löwy argue that the three parameters of Marxist analysis used by Nimni "is a caricature of Marx's thought" (1990: 133). Specifically, they argue against the notion that Marxism is Eurocentric, and that capitalism, as the then most advanced European economic system, is revolutionary and progressive throughout the world. Drawing upon the ambiguous statements in Marx and Engels—where they argue, for example, both that capitalism had swept away reactionary systems in Algeria and India and that the spread of capitalism unleashed some of the worst horrors ever witnessed—Traverso and Löwy conclude that Marx was neither Eurocentric nor, relatedly, committed to a vision of historical development as passing through inevitable stages (1990: 134–35). They point to the famous 1881 letter to Vera Zasulich in which Marx held out the hope that the cooperative peasant communes in Russia could allow it to move directly from feudalism to socialism (Traverso and Löwy 1990: 134–35), a position he could not have taken if he held rigidly to a concept of inevitable development.

Hoffman and Mzala (1991) address a specific issue raised by Nimni, one of critical importance to understanding the left's position on the Aboriginal question. This is the argument found in Engels that there are progressive nations whose national aspirations are to be supported; and there are "non-historic nations," who are not destined to develop on the same trajectory as England, France and Germany, and whose national aspirations will not further the coming of the proletarian revolution. Nimni argues that, for Engels, "non-historic" nations are those too small to support nationally based bourgeoisies. Hence, these national entities can survive only if they revert to social and political relations that are essentially feudal or backward (Nimni 1989: 312). Hoffman and Mzala ask whether these comments of Engels, which have "understandably embarrassed Marxist writers," are logically derived from the core of Marxist thought or are mere interjections that can be rejected without having to abandon Marxism (1991: 420–21).

Hoffman and Mzala are clear that, in their opinion, these were abstract and non-dialectical arguments inconsistent with the general thrust of the Marxist corpus. In fact, Engels himself admitted in the last years of his life that he and Marx had on occasion overstated the dependence of historical change on purely economic and technological processes (Hoffman and Mzala 1991: 421). Hoffman and Mzala emphasize that, for Marx, arguments regarding the general patterns of historical development—from technologically less-developed to technologically more-developed, for example—are just that, general patterns. *Most* societies seem to follow this pattern; not all do, nor should they; "while Marx and Engels consistently regarded economic conditions as the factor which ultimately determines historical development, they equally acknowledged the multiplicity of causes or determinations operating on historical outcomes" (Hoffman and Mzala 1991: 411). Importantly, nationhood is included among these other factors (Hoffman and Mzala 1991: 412). Marxist analyses cannot simply examine the economic base of a national grouping, pass judgement on its viability as the ground for an indigenous bourgeoisie and then, on this basis, support or not support the nation's right to self-determination.

The importance of this issue politically and programmatically can be seen when we examine the national question as played out in Canada. Canada has a minority who for various reasons does not feel part of the national whole. The country has, as well, a history that is marked by forcible inclusion of peoples into the state. In Canada, both the French-speaking settlers and the various Aboriginal nations were forcibly included. The province of Quebec eventually agreed to a partnership with the English-speaking majority under the terms of *British North America Act* of 1867, and although this agreement was extracted under some pressure there was an element of consent. Aboriginal nations in Canada were never asked for their consent. They became part of Canada under questionable legal circumstances, without consultation and often without even prior notification.

Is Nimni (1989) correct in arguing that Marxism has a clear, analytical formula for dealing with specific "national questions"? In the concrete case of national tensions in Canada, does the left have an algorithm that it can apply in formulating policy on the question of a right to self-determination for Quebec and Aboriginal nations? The interpretation of the theoretical underpinnings of the Marxist position on the national question proposed by Nimni answers this question positively. If one accepts the analysis of Marx's historical materialism as provided by Nimni—an analysis accepted by significant sections of the left in Canada—then one is committed to the view that Aboriginal nations' quest for self-determination is not to be supported because they are "non-historic" nations. They are not economically viable sovereign entities that can develop a local bourgeoisie.

If the left were to follow through on the consequences of the analysis offered by Hoffman and Mzala (1991), the question of the right of Aboriginal nations to self-determination becomes more complex because it is more firmly rooted in specific historical and political circumstances. On this reading of Marx, proper policy decisions cannot be made on the basis of an abstract, formulaic understanding of relationships between economic and political processes. Rather, the left must address the concrete political needs of specific conditions. So, for example, the claim to the right of national self-determination by the Mohawk nation would have to be evaluated according to a variety of political, historical and economic factors. These factors are significantly different from those, for example, of the Afrikaner nation in post-apartheid South Africa, which is also asserting the right to national self-determination. The former is the victim of years of oppression, the latter the perpetrator of oppression. The very different histories of these two peoples, and the different consequences following from this right, mean that the left would have to evaluate each according to a great variety of considerations. If, however, one were to employ the reading of Marx found in Nimni (1989), then the left would not support the Mohawk claim because that nation is not economically and technologically developed enough to support a bourgeois class. It is just such reasoning that has led many on the left to reject such claims to sovereignty and national self-determination.

The best developed example of a Marxist analysis of the national question that invokes political and historical criteria as critical is found in Lenin's writings on the national question. The principle that infuses all the twists and turns of Lenin's position is his belief that, although nationalism tends to separate people and fragment working-class struggle, to deny a nation's nationalist aspirations is itself a form of national chauvinism. The emergence of capitalism world-wide produces two seemingly contradictory tendencies. The first is a growing sense of national identity and a struggle for independence within which a national economy can flourish. This tendency can often be overlaid with racist and chauvinist overtones. The world has witnessed just such national movements in all their complexity in the breakup of the former Yugoslavia, where the struggle for the freedom from national oppression often results in its continuation as the newly formed nation in turn oppresses its new minority groups. The second tendency is the growth of internationalism as the formal barriers that separate people are overcome by the speed of commerce and industry and by international solidarity. Here the tendency of capitalism to spread globally renders nugatory the formal boundaries between peoples as well as their cultural and linguistic differences. Hence, the struggle of Aboriginal peoples in Canada for autonomy must not only face the difficulties of finding a way to achieve legal sovereignty, it must also find ways to avoid being homogenized into a world capitalist culture.

Lenin's position on the national question tries to take account of both tendencies. A Marxist position on the right of national self-determination must advocate

> firstly, the equality of nations and languages and the impermissibility of all *privileges* in these respect (and also the right of nations to self-determination, with which we shall deal separately later); secondly, the principle of internationalism and uncompromising struggle against contamination of the proletariat with bourgeois nationalism, even of the most refined kind. (Lenin 1971: 15)

In a sense, though, this position does not do more than reproduce the contradictory tendencies of the evolution of capitalism. Lenin's position has a "Canadian" flavour: national autonomy if necessary, but not necessarily national autonomy. While no oppression of national groups can be tolerated by the left, and while all chauvinisms must be countered even it means secession by the oppressed nation, the proper outlook of the working class is internationalist. Here, Lenin is following the Marxism dictum that the worker has no national home. The proletariat of Russia must not take up arms against the proletariat of Germany.

Let us look at two important examples of national movements and Lenin's response to them. From these can be gleaned the conceptual core of his views. In 1905 the Norwegian parliament resolved that it would no longer recognize the sovereignty of Sweden over Norway. It held a plebiscite in which the majority of Norwegians voted to separate from Sweden and form a sovereign state, which was soon after peacefully recognized by Sweden. The secession was peaceful, Lenin noted approvingly, despite the strenuous objections of Sweden's ruling landed proprietors, who favoured forcible retention of Norway, because the Swedish working class overcame all appeals to Swedish nationalism and chauvinism and supported the right of Norway to separate (Lenin 1971: 68–73).

The second example is the debate between Lenin and Rosa Luxemburg, one of the founders of the Communist Party in Germany, over the question of the secessionist movement in Poland. The issue of the debate was the meaning and value of the clause in the program of the Russian Marxists which called for the right of all nations to self-determination. Lenin defended the clause, arguing that it must mean that all nations have the right to form separate, independent states. Specifically, does the Polish nation have the right—to be supported by the left—to separate from the Russian empire and form an independent state? Lenin supported, and Luxemburg opposed, Polish independence. Luxemburg's arguments were largely economic reasons. Poland's uniting with Russia led to a highly interconnected economy and a much more rapid industrialization and development of capitalism than would have been possible in Poland alone (Lenin 1971: 47). A huge national entity like Russia provided opportunities to exploit an enormous market, something not available to smaller entities. Furthermore, the nationalist movement within Poland (and in other nations striving for national independence) was led by local bourgeoisie. Therefore, supporting the right to independence and national self-determination amounted to supporting the nationalist aspirations, and ruling aspirations, of the local bourgeoisie (Lenin 1971: 58).

Lenin's responses to Luxemburg are revealing because they were guided by political considerations much more than by any acceptance of an economic determinism. In answer to Luxemburg's first point, Lenin wrote:

> From their daily experience the masses know perfectly well the value of geographical and economic ties and the advantages of a big market and a big state. They will, therefore, resort to secession only when national oppression and national friction make joint life absolutely intolerable and hinder any and all economic intercourse. In that case, the interests of capitalist development and of the freedom of the class struggle will be best served by secession. (1971 66)

This can be decided only by the oppressed nation itself. Not granting the right of self-determination, and not supporting it rigorously, can lead to friction between workers of the oppressor and the oppressed nation, making international working-class solidarity more difficult. In the same vein, not giving full support to the right to independence is often tantamount to supporting the privileges of their own oppressing bourgeoisie.

For Lenin, the important issue was always to analyze politically the interests of the working class. For example, he wrote:

> *Insofar* as the bourgeoisie of the oppressed nation fights the oppressor, we are always, in every case, and more strongly than anyone else, *in favour*, for we are the staunchest and the most consistent enemies of oppression. But insofar as the bourgeoisie of the oppressed nation stands for *its own* bourgeois nationalism, we stand against. We fight against the privileges and violence of the oppressor nation, and do not in any way condone strivings for privileges on the part of the oppressed nation. (Lenin 1971: 55)

The rationale for Lenin's position is that despite identifiable tendencies for the formation of large nation-states as the appropriate political arrangement for the emergence of capitalism, and despite the "progressive" nature of such entities, concrete political questions of the international solidarity of the working class and opposition to national chauvinisms and oppression must take precedence. This means giving unilateral support for the right of nations to form separate states, even capitalist states. It does not mean ceasing to struggle against a new bourgeoisie should it emerge.

Conflicting Readings

We argue that current analysis and policy positions given by the left are based on three arguments or readings of Marx. These are not uncontested readings. In fact, alternative interpretations of Marx can lead to quite different positions on the Aboriginal question. For the purposes of shorthand, these contested readings can be referred to as technological determinism versus the primacy of class struggle; the inevitability of historical stages versus historical openness; and the fetishizing of consumption versus the central importance of the concept of alienation.

The left in Canada, especially the Marxist-based left, has to a very significant degree based its position on the view that Marxism advocates technological determinism, that is, that the dialectic of history, the underlying development that drives social change, is the continuing development of the technologies of production. Most frequently quoted is the passage in which Marx wrote:

> Social relations are closely bound up with productive forces. In acquiring new productive forces men change their mode of pro-

> duction; and in changing their mode of production, in changing their way of earning their living, they change all their social relations. The hand-mill gives you society with the feudal lord; the steam-mill, society with the industrial capitalist. (Marx and Engels 1975: 166)

This argument is succinct and seductive. The technology of production at a specific stage necessarily engenders social relations around the productive process. For example, relationships between people will be different in a shop producing tableware by craft production methods than if the same goods were produced in a highly automated factory. Furthermore, these social relations of production will have important consequences for the political structures of a society. The conclusion, therefore, is that economic, social, political and even ideological structures are built on the foundation of relations of production, which are themselves determined by the technologies employed. A change in technology has significant consequences. The difference between feudalism and capitalism, to put the matter most starkly, hinges on the different technologies of each era.

As we have seen, closely tied to the argument for technological determinism is the view of history as passing through a definite set of stages. Marx argued in *The German Ideology* that human history is composed of five distinct periods, each marked by different forms of production; they are tribal, ancient communal or slave, feudal, capitalist and, finally, socialism and communism (Marx and Engels 1966: 9–14). Each form evolves out of its preceding form as new methods of production develop. Two examples, one theoretical, the other practical, demonstrate the hold that this schematization of history has had on Marxist scholars and practitioners. At the level of theoretical analysis, much controversy has been engendered by the occasional references that Marx made to the Asiatic Mode of Production as a social form unique to certain Asian societies, especially India. Interpreters have been led to ask if these references mean that the periodization of history proposed in *The German Ideology* was superceded by Marx in his later writings. If so, does this mean that there was an inherent flaw in the logic of the inevitable replacement of one mode of life by another as the internal contradictions of the earlier gave way to later, more developed forms? Or, is the Asiatic Mode merely a variant of the feudal, thus allowing the necessary historical stages to remain unchanged? The debates over appropriate revolutionary tactics, which occurred between Lenin, Stalin and Trotsky within the Bolshevik Party prior to the Russian Revolution in 1917 involved similar theoretical issues. Stalin argued that the party should follow a two-stage approach to revolution. Since Russia was still largely feudal, Stalin, adhering to a belief in the necessity of history passing through the stages detailed by Marx, argued that the Bolsheviks should encourage a bourgeois, not a socialist, revolution because Russia could only become socialist after it had become capitalist, which was in keeping with the Marxian periodization of history. That this argument was ultimately defeated within the Party by Trotsky, with Lenin's backing, does not alter the significance attached to the notion of necessary stages of history found in Marx.

These two related concepts constitute a reading of Marx that is close to that articulated by Nimni (1989) in his analysis of Marx on the national question, and it is foundational to the left's positions on the Aboriginal question. If iron laws of history appear to be unfolding as technological developments are generated continually to expand the processes of production, then there is little room for the development of an autonomous and traditional Aboriginal economy or society. The failure to give full, unconditional support for the self-determination of Aboriginal nations by the left in Canada is an example of consigning the "non-historic" nations to inevitable absorption into the more modern, "historic" nations. As Nimni (1989) pointed out, this interpretation of the national question is based on a reading of history as economically determined and inevitable.

Furthermore the left groups examined appear to be mesmerized by the possibilities for and ethic of consumption, which is held out in mature capitalist societies such as Canada as the key criterion of the good life. Marx certainly was critical of capitalism because of its impoverishment of the working class, which was so widespread in the 1800s. Engels (1844) wrote of the horrible conditions in Manchester in *The Condition of the Working Class in England in 1844*. The drive for profits left the workers bereft of any material comfort, and Marx foresaw that socialism would result in much greater possibilities for consumption and a much higher living standard for the working class. Based on this, the left in Canada has argued that a capitalist economy, let alone socialism, is superior to traditional economies because of the vastly greater capacity it has for the satisfaction of need. Capitalist economies, quite simply, can produce more goods and so will ultimately command the allegiance of Aboriginal persons over any attachment to a traditional economy and culture.

The fact that many Aboriginal persons choose to remain on reserve, living outside of the mainstream economy in a lower standard of living, is explained by the racism of Canadian society. That is, they are excluded from participating as proletarians by such endemic racism. Their failure to embrace, in any significant way, the manner of life of the mainstream is not seen as a preference for a traditional life, as this preference results in a lower living standard. The motivations which account for the psychology of the typical person in a capitalist economy—that to consume more is to live better—is assumed to be true for Aboriginal persons as well, and their isolation is not seen as a rational choice. Hence, for the left the key problem facing Aboriginal communities is their (racist) exclusion from the mainstream. The promise held out to them by the left is a future in which their inevitable assimilation into a modern, progressive economy will be eased by socialism's removal of racist barriers. The focus on racism is logically derived from the belief that the appropriate future of Aboriginal cultures in North America is eventual incorporation into the melting pot of modernity and eventual reduction to the status of just one more piece of the multicultural jigsaw puzzle.

As we have noted, the reading of Marx underlying the left's present analysis is not the only one. In fact, it has undergone severe challenge as various interpreters have questioned it as an appropriate understanding of Marx. Max Horkheimer, Theodor Adorno and Herbert Marcuse have questioned the economic determinism of this interpretation, arguing instead that cultural aspects, especially ideological constructions, have enormous impact on the evolution of society. Their concern, like that of Antonio Gramsci, was why revolution had not broken out in Europe by the mid-1930s when the forces of production had become fully developed and worker impoverishment was widespread. According to Marxist tradition—especially from the strand of Marx's thought in which one finds the arguments of historical inevitability and economic determinism—the conditions for revolution were clearly present. And yet no revolution came. Instead, Europe was buried under the weight of fascist rule. The answer must be that other factors besides economic ones determined historical development. As a result, an alternative reading of Marx emerged into mainstream Marxist commentary, which stressed the multiplicity of factors shaping historical evolution, particularly ideological and political factors. The remainder of this chapter briefly discusses aspects of this alternative reading.

Greater emphasis on political and ideological aspects of society helps highlight the importance of class struggle as a driving force in history. There is certainly much evidence in Marx's work that he saw the tensions and eventual open conflict between the subordinate and superordinate classes as the key to history. The opening paragraphs of the *Communist Manifesto* include the famous line: "The history of all hitherto existing society is the history of class struggles." Marx continues:

> Freeman and slave, patrician and plebeian, lord and serf, guild-master and journeyman, in a word, oppressor and oppressed, stood in constant opposition to one another, carried on an uninterrupted, now hidden, now open fight, a fight that each time ended, either in

> a revolutionary re-constitution of society at large, or in the common ruin of the contending classes. (1978: 469–70)

Every social formation in which productive property is held privately is determined in its main features by the character of the struggle between the class of persons who own property and the class that does not. If the owners of the means of production are to continue in their privileged position in the face of a mass who are under their subjugation, they must constitute the political, judicial, military, educational, legal and ideological institutions and practices of society necessary to support and maintain this privilege.

Take, for example, the issue of work and the labouring process. Here we can see clearly the difference between an analysis that places technological change at the forefront and one that places class struggle at the forefront. Commentators on the evolution of the labour process, on the day-to-day practices of factory production, have offered two quite different explanations to account for the changes in this process over the past century. Some, like Taylor, have argued that continual refinements in the techniques of production have made the productive process more efficient. Fewer and fewer workers are needed and the nature of work itself has become less skilled and more automated. The drive behind these "improvements" is the drive towards greater technological efficiency as companies compete for markets and profits. Others, such as Herbert Gintis, see the increased use of technology not as motivated by a desire for greater efficiency but as a way of controlling a recalcitrant and often antagonistic labour force. Technologies are themselves created and used as instruments in class struggle as overseers try to find ways to isolate workers from each other and lower their value as their skills are no longer needed. This is an interesting example because on this argument the technology itself is seen as determined by class struggle. Rather than being an autonomous force of historical change, technology, like other factors, is shaped by the contention between classes.

Because the driving force of history is class struggle, which is decisively operative in the political sphere, history does not follow an inevitable path but is open to the vicissitudes of human practice. Not only is there an openness to history in this reading—it may be possible for a state to jump from feudalism to socialism, for example, as Russia did in 1917—but more traditional social and economic forms are no longer necessarily doomed to extinction. Because class struggle is political, because it requires the mobilization of workers consciously committed to a program of social change, its direction (and the direction of history in general) is much more open.

The final aspect of the alternate reading involves the motivations that stimulate class struggle. In the *Economic and Philosophic Manuscripts of 1844*

Marx argued that the defining experience for workers under capitalism was not poverty but alienation. Without underestimating the terrible effects of the poverty of the working class in the 1800s, Marx saw that the essential, or defining, property of life under capitalism was alienation at work. It is through labour that humankind expresses itself and creates itself. Through it, culture is created and different ways of life emerge. Aboriginal cultures see spiritual value in the land because the land is the source of life, and their culture involves working with and through the land. Marx wrote:

> First, the fact that labour is *external* to the worker, i.e., it does not belong to his intrinsic nature; that in his work, therefore, he does not affirm himself but denies himself, does not feel content but unhappy, does not develop freely his physical and mental energy but mortifies his body and ruins his mind. The worker therefore only feels himself outside his work, and in his work feels outside himself. He feels at home when he is not working, and when he is working he does not feel at home. His labour is therefore not voluntary, but coerced; it is *forced labour*. It is therefore not the satisfaction of a need; it is merely a *means* to satisfy needs external to it. Its alien character emerges clearly in the fact that as soon as no physical or other compulsion exists, labour is shunned like the plague. External labour, labour in which man alienates himself, is a labour of self-sacrifice, of mortification. Lastly, the external character of labour for the worker appears in the fact that it is not his own, but someone else's, that it does not belong to him, that in it he belongs, not to himself, but to another. (1977: 71)

Furthermore, even an increase in the standard of living does not mean that the de-humanizing effects of alienated work will be overcome. Even well-paid factory work requires the worker to sell his or her very life in exchange for things. Not only Marx, but such diverse thinkers as Plato and Henry David Thoreau saw this as a pact with the devil. Traditional peoples who have experienced non-alienated labour must be forced into factories and mines. Indeed, Marx argued further that,

> An enforced *increase of wages* (disregarding all other difficulties, including the fact that it would only be by force, too, that such an increase, being an anomaly, could be maintained) would therefore be nothing but better *payment for the slave*, and would not win either for the worker or for labour their human status and dignity.
>
> Indeed, even the *equality of wages*, as demanded by Proudhon, only transforms the relationship of the present-day worker to his

> labour into the relationship of all men to labour. Society is then conceived as an abstract capitalist. (1997: 78)

Even though Aboriginal communities and their traditional economies may not be as productive as present-day capitalist economies, or even future socialist ones that employ factory labour, they may attempt to resist modernity because the price (alienated labour) seems too high. The offer of being liberated in the revolutionary overthrow of capitalism at the cost of becoming proletarianized is not necessarily appealing. Marx's tragic sense at the demise of traditional cultures was based on his simultaneous sympathy for the life of traditional societies and his recognition that, despite the pain of their destruction, there was hope for redemption in the eventual emergence of a socialist alternative. For those on the brink of destruction this is only passing comfort.

PROSPECTS FOR THE FUTURE

The relationship between Aboriginal communities and the Canadian state has been marked by a series of crises, from the confrontation at Oka to the legal decision and subsequent maneuverings of the Marshall case and its aftermath. Governments of the day, both federal and provincial, have consistently failed to deal with Aboriginal communities in a generous spirit. Time and again opportunities to construct a more hopeful relationship, one which holds out the promise that centuries of oppression may be coming to an end, have been lost. Antagonism by the government is exacerbated by racism from the citizenry. Preserving a traditional life has been rendered difficult by the pressures of an ever-expanding modern economy. Even for those Aboriginal persons who embrace the values and ambitions of modern life, however, the road is not easy. Unemployment is astronomical, largely because the endemic racism of Canadian society makes finding work and assimilating into the mainstream very difficult. It is not uncommon to survey towns near reserve communities and find almost no one from the reserve with a job in the town. This is the reality for most Aboriginal persons in Canada today. The material conditions, resources and skills needed to live in some approximation of a traditional material culture are not available for most communities; and there are few opportunities for assimilation. The result is the present situation of unemployment, welfare and poverty. Compounding the poverty is the difficult question of how to live. To what extent is preserving traditional life a worthy goal? If it is an important part of living well for many Aboriginal persons, then how can it be achieved? What steps and strategies will ensure that what is Aboriginal will not disappear?

These are not easy questions to answer nor easy choices to make. The silence of the left has made matters worse. For example, the text on the history of the Communist Party in Canada (Avakumovic 1975) makes no mention of the Aboriginal issue. For parties on the left, the fate of Aboriginal peoples and the fate of a traditional culture confronted by a capitalist economy is of little interest. When they have addressed these questions the responses have not been satisfactory to Aboriginal communities and, as a result, there has been no interaction or mutual support. This is surprising and lamentable because both the left and Aboriginal communities are struggling against the oppression of people that results from a modern, capitalist economy.

The left's silence is due significantly to the way in which they have conceptualized the historical dynamic of capitalism. Their understanding of history and of the inevitability of certain key attributes of modernity render their goals and tactics incommensurate with the Aboriginal struggle to preserve traditional life. As we have seen, the left's analysis of contemporary society and events is grounded on an acceptance of the key concept associated with modernity—the fact and value of progress. Modern cultures, the inheritors of the Enlightenment, see history as a development or progress from less advanced to more advanced forms. History is marked by continual improvements in science and technology. Knowing is no longer thought of as contemplation of the meaning of being. Rather, it is equated with the capacity to manipulate and transform. Philosophic insight is being replaced by technological mastery as the model of human understanding. Scientists, philosophers and social commentators all are impressed by the power of technologies and technological reasoning to transform our environing world, to make it more amenable to human purposes. Progress in such knowing has seemed inevitable. This is especially visible as our capacity to produce and consume is directly linked to technological and scientific progress.

In this general atmosphere, the left all too frequently has infused its own understandings and policies with the ideals of modernity, especially that of progress. Like many inheritors of the Enlightenment, the left has read its own intellectual antecedents through these categories. Just as it sees its own victory as part of a necessary historical development, so too it sees history in terms of stages. Definitive of the evolutionary epochs are qualitative developments in technology. The present system of capitalist relations is progressive because it spreads the more advanced forms of production (and increased consumption) throughout the world. Whatever stands in the way of progress is condemned as reactionary because it is an impediment to the emergence of newer and better social forms and even more powerful means of manipulating nature and satisfying our desire to consume.

Acceptance of the Enlightenment project infuses the left's political stands on the Aboriginal question, and it conditions their reading of Marx.

This is particularly evident in the issue of the right of Aboriginal nations to self-determination. In general, the left in Canada does not support the right of Aboriginal nations to form sovereign entities because it believes that self-determination is progressive, and hence to be supported, only if the creation of a sovereign jurisdiction helps develop an indigenous bourgeoisie. If it does not then national aspirations are not supported by the left. Traditional economies are seen as doomed relics of the past, destined to become extinct. They impede progress and economic development. That they should gain the legitimacy and jurisdictional support that follows from Aboriginal national sovereignty should not be encouraged.

The silence of the left and its failure to support rigorously Aboriginal aspirations has been detrimental to the latter's struggle for justice. Even though the Canadian left has not been strong electorally, its influence has been important in determining the direction of public policy throughout Canadian history, such as the introduction of medicare. Its failure to defend Aboriginal rights and to make the preservation of traditional culture a priority has allowed the Canadian public to ignore the assault on Aboriginal peoples and cultures. Furthermore, these issues have never become an important part of public discourse. There is no political cost for neglecting Aboriginal issues, no fallout for celebrating the arrival on Turtle Island of invaders who murdered, enslaved and brutalized millions. We can celebrate Columbus and memorialize the dispossessors of Aboriginal peoples without a murmur of protest. The silence of the left has greatly exacerbated a general toleration of abuse.

The left need not ignore this fight for survival. It need not be committed to the project of modernity, to a faith in the beneficence of ever more technology and consumption. While Marx embraces certain key elements of the Enlightenment worldview, he clearly rejects others. Most centrally, he recognizes that the increased commodification of human relationships, and of all aspects of social life, means that we are increasingly alienated from the core of our being. Marx, more than any other thinker, seeks to deconstruct the naturalness of the commodity form and the modes of production that typify modern capitalist life. He laments the loss of traditional cultures even if he does not see a way beyond their destruction. The left should take up the obligation to defend and to struggle alongside those who wish to preserve Aboriginal traditions because it is a cause that is worthy of support. No one and no group on the left can be so certain of the trajectory of history that a noble cause is abandoned because it does not fit an abstract model.

The left need not choose between two alternatives of what amounts to a false dichotomy. The present policies and strategies do not demand that we choose either accepting the direction of history and following through on stages that Marx envisaged or supporting a reactionary, backward-looking Aboriginal nationalism and traditionalism. These need not be mutually exclusive, as the left has often hypothesized. The demand for the preservation of Aboriginal traditional life can have progressive, even revolutionary, consequences. It is difficult to imagine how a viable traditional material culture could be sustained in present circumstances. Without romanticizing traditional economic life, it is possible to preserve what would amount to functional equivalents of traditional economic practices in a modern context. Hunting, fishing and farming can still provide important economic activities for many communities. These can be supplemented by cooperative activities, such as housing and infrastructure construction, education, social care and wholesale and retail outlets.

Developments such as these, however, would require significant, progressive changes in the present capitalist economy and in Canadian political life. First of all, control over large sections of resources would have to be handed over to Aboriginal communities. Crown lands, fishing rights and farm lands would all have to be put under Aboriginal control in sufficient quantities to make their communities viable. Second, if Aboriginal peoples are to gain a significant measure of their livelihood from the land, there must be land and water available that can be used. This means that environmental preservation must become the first priority. The Maliseet people lived by catching salmon spawning in the Saint John River. This river is now dammed. There is a large pulp mill at its mouth, mills up and down its length, pesticide-laden farms line its shores and the stream beds that feed it are being blocked because of clear-cutting. Economic development has destroyed the river as a resource for traditional material culture. The democratic, human right of a people to preserve their culture would, if acted upon, require Canadian society to pull back from its destruction of the environment. Forests, rivers, oceans are the basis of life for Aboriginal communities. Respect for the survival of traditional cultures means that the modern urge for progress must be tempered. It does not mean, as some on the left have claimed, that we will all go back to living in teepees. Relentless, limitless, unmoderated development, however, will have to be stopped, and in some cases reversed. Ironically, this may be the only hope for survival of modern, Western society itself.

Even these relatively small changes will be very difficult to accomplish. It is hard to envision a dam being removed, control over a crown forest being handed over to an Aboriginal community or environmental degradation being halted. Aboriginal peoples do not have the social force required to effect these changes. They must have the support of the advanced, progressive elements of labour. To date, the left has done nothing to rally organized labour to support the right of Aboriginal peoples to survive. In fact, they have unwittingly contributed to the continued antagonism by juxtaposing development and jobs against tradition.

Furthermore, nationalist sentiment in Canada, and support for the process of nation-building, also pits labour and the left against the interests of Aboriginal peoples. Traditionally, nation-building and Canadian nationalism have been equated with such development initiatives as the construction of a trans-Canada railway by John A. MacDonald and the "settling" of the Prairies and the turning of it into farmland. These actions helped to create a national economy, one that binds Canada together and maintains our separateness from the United States. As such, these actions have historically had support that cuts across all class lines. Important sections of the Canadian left are fervent Canadian nationalists. Aboriginal people have been driven almost to extinction by nation-building. They cannot survive much more of it.

Insofar as the left lends support and credibility to nation-building and the continued development of the Canadian economy, it is (unwittingly) contributing to the destruction of Aboriginal peoples. Economic development undermines the ecological and social spaces within which traditional cultures can thrive. Furthermore, such development, and the nationalist interpretation given to it, legitimates the ideas of progress and the superiority of modern over traditional forms of life, and it justifies assimilation and dispossession.

The consequences of the left and labour adopting the standpoint of economic nationalism and development have been bad for them as well as for Aboriginal communities. The ideologies of consumption, of Canadian chauvinism, of ever more technological progress are clearly antithetical to Aboriginal tradition, but they are also key ways that bourgeois values and social and economic practices are normalized. The economic relationships that exploit and alienate workers are made to seem inevitable, natural, even good, in large part by being linked with other secondary ideas like the ethic of consumption or Canadian nationalism. In this way, the real effects on workers are hidden from them. Support for the preservation of Aboriginal traditional culture will help illuminate the real consequences of a chauvinistic nation-building. As David Muga (1988: 39) has written:

> The interests of a popular alliance do not counterpoise a worker's movement and ethnosocial formation as competitive organs for overall political leadership of emancipatory struggles. The fight against the imperialistic tendencies of a capitalist economic order requires political unity and an understanding of the ultimate link between self-determination of an ethnoformation and workers' class emancipation. Neither are isolatable factors.

REFERENCES

Adams, Howard. 1984. "Marxism and Native Americans." *American Indian Culture and Research Journal* 8, 4.

_____. 1995. *A Tortured People: The Politics of Colonization*. Penticton: Theytus.

Alfred, Gerald. 1995. *Heeding the Voices of Our Ancestors*. Toronto: Oxford.

Anders, Gary. 1980. "Theories of Underdevelopment and the American Indian." *Journal of Economic Issues* 14, 3 (September).

Avakumovic, Ivan. 1975. *The Communist Party in Canada: A History*. Toronto: McClelland.

Avineri, Shlomo. 1990. "Toward a Socialist Theory of Nationalism." *Dissent* 37 (Fall).

Barreiro, José, ed. 1992. *Indian Roots of American Democracy*. Ithaca: Akwe Kon.

Barron, F. Laurie. 1997. *Walking in Indian Moccasins: The Native Policies of Tommy Douglas and the CCF*. Vancouver: UBC Press.

Barsh, Russell Lawrence. 1988. "Contemporary Marxist Theory and Native American Reality." *American Indian Quarterly* 12, 3 (Summer): 187–211.

Bear Nicholas, Andrea. 1994. "Mascarene's Treaty of 1725." *UNB Law Journal* 43, 43.

Bedford, David, and Sidney Pobihushchy. 1995. "On-Reserve Status Indian Voter Participation in the Maritimes." *The Canadian Journal of Native Studies* 15, 2.

Bedford, David, and Thom Workman. 1997. "The Great Law of Peace: Alternative Inter-Nation(al) Practices and the Iroquoian Confederacy." *Alternatives* 22.

Berger, Thomas. 1985. *Village Journey*. New York: Hill and Wang.

_____. 1991. *A Long and Terrible Shadow: White Values, Native Rights in the Americas*. Toronto: Douglas and McIntyre.

Biesick, Chas. 1966. "What the Palefaces Have to Learn from the Indians." *The Commonwealth* 26, 3.

Black Elk, Frank. 1983. "Observation on Marxism and Lakota Traditions." In W. Churchill (ed.), *Marxism and Native Americans*. Boston: South End.

Christjohn, Roland. 1998. Public Lecture. St. Thomas University. Fredericton, New Brunswick.

Churchill, Ward. 1983. "Journeying Toward a Debate." In W. Churchill (ed.), *Marxism and Native Americans*. Boston: South End.

Communist Party of Canada. 1977. *The Road to Socialism in Canada*. Toronto: Communist Party of Canada.

_____. 1982. *Canada's Party of Socialism: The History of the Communist Party of Canada. 1921–1976*. Toronto: Progress.

Deloria, Vine. 1983. "Circling the Same Old Rock." In W. Churchill (ed.), *Marxism and Native Americans*. Boston: South End.

Douglas, Tommy. 1967. "Douglas Fights to Preserve Indian and Eskimo Services." *The Commonwealth* 28, 14.

_____. 1968. "Urgent Need to Meet Problems of the Indians of Canada." *The Commonwealth* 28, 23.

Dugre, Michel, and Robert Simms. 1990. "Canada: Behind the Struggle of Native Peoples in History of Racism, Part 1." *The Militant* 54, 32.

Dyck, Noel. 1997. *Differing Visions: Administering Indian Residential Schooling in Prince Alberta 1867–1995*. Halifax: Fernwood.

Engels, Frederick. 1968. "The French Rule in Algeria." In S. Avineri (ed.), *Karl Marx in Colonialism and Modernization*. Garden City: Doubleday.

_____. 1974. *The Condition of the Working Class in England in 1844*. London: Panther.

_____. 1979. "Letter to Kautsky, February 16, 1884." In K. Marx and F. Engels, *Pre-Capitalist Economic Formations*. Moscow: Progress.

_____. 1983. *The Origin of the Family, Private Property and the State in the Light of the Researches of Lewis H. Morgan*. Moscow: Progress.

Etkin, Carol. 1988. "The Sechelt Indian Band: An Analysis of a New Form of Native Self Government." *Canadian Journal of Native Studies* 8, 1.

Flanagan, Tom. 1998. "Native Sovereignty: Does Anyone Really Want an Aboriginal Archipelago?" In Mark Charlton and Paul Barker (eds.), *Crosscurrents: Contemporary Political Issues*. Toronto: Nelson.

Fletcher, Paula. 1981. "Northern Development and Native Peoples." *Communist Viewpoint* 13, 2.

Fluehr-Lobban, Carolyn. 1979. "A Marxist Reappraisal of the Matriarchate." *Current Anthropology* 20, 2 (June).

Frideres, James. 1998. *Aboriginal Peoples in Canada: Contemporary Conflicts*. Scarborough: Prentice Hall Allyn and Bacon Canada.

Gintis, Herbert. 1976. "The Nature of Labor Exchange and the Theory of Capitalist Production." *Review of Radical Political Economics* 8, 2.

Great Law of Peace. 1973. Akwesasne: White Roots of Peace.

Hegel, G.W.F. 1956. *The Philosophy of History*. New York: Dover.

Hendrickson, Marvin. 1976. "The Native Challenge to the NDP." *The*

Commonwealth 36, 20.

Hoffman, John, and Nxumala Mzala. 1991. "'Non-Historic Nations' and the National Question: A South African Perspective." *Science and Society* 54, 4 (Winter).

Horkheimer, Max, and Theodor Adorno. 1972. *Dialectic of Enlightenment*. New York: Continuum.

Internal Bulletin [of the International Socialists] "Quebec, Native Rights and the National Question in Canada." 1996. November 21, 3.

Johansen, Bruce. 1982. *Forgotten Founders*. Ipswich: Gambit.

Karoniaktajeh. n.d. *A Warrior's Hand Book*. Pamphlet.

Kashton, William. 1977. "A Principled Approach to the National Question." *Communist Viewpoint* 9,3.

Knockwood, Isabelle. 1992. *Out of the Depths*. Lockeport: Roseway.

Krader, Lawrence. 1974. *The Ethnological Notebooks of Karl Marx*. Assen: Van Gorcum.

Leacock, Eleanor. 1954. "The Montagnais 'Hunting Territory' and the Fur Trade." *American Anthropological Association* 56, 5.

Lenin, V.I. 1971. *Critical Remarks on the National Question and The Right of Nations to Self- Determination*. Moscow: Progress.

Marx, Karl. 1965. *Pre-Capitalist Economic Formations*. New York: International.

_____. 1968a. "The British Rule in India." In S. Avineri (ed.), *Karl Marx on Colonialism and Modernization*. Garden City: Doubleday.

_____. 1968b. "The Future of British Rule in India." In S. Avineri (ed.), *Karl Marx on Colonialism and Modernization*. Garden City: Doubleday.

_____ 1977. *Economic and Philosophic Manuscripts of 1844*. Moscow: Progress.

_____. 1978. "The Communist Manifesto." In Robert Tucker (ed.), *The Marx-Engels Reader*. New York: Norton.

Marx, Karl, and Friedrick Engels. 1966. *The German Ideology*. New York: International.

_____. 1975. "The Poverty of Philosophy. " *Collected Works, VI*. New York: International.

Means, Russell. 1983. "Same Old Song." In W. Churchill (ed.), *Marxism and Native Americans*. Boston: South End.

Militant. 1992. "Fight for National Rights of Quebecois and Natives." In *Militant* supplement: *International Socialist Review*. 56, 21.

Monture-Angus, Patricia. 1999. *Journeying Forward: Dreaming First Nations' Independence*. Halifax: Fernwood.

Morgan, Lewis Henry. 1962. *League of the Iroquois*. New York: Citadel.

_____. 1964. *Ancient Society*. Cambridge: Belknop.

Muga, David A. 1988. "Native Americans and the Nationalities Question: Premises for a Marxist Approach to Ethnicity and Self-Determination." *Journal of Ethnic Studies* 16 (1).

Nimni, Ephraim. 1989. "Marx, Engels and the National Question." *Science and Society* 53, 3 (Fall).

Nofz, Michael. 1987. "Treading Upon Separate Paths: Native American Ideology and Marxist Analysis." *Sociological Inquiry* 57 (Summer).

Novack, George. 1992. *Genocide Against the Indians.* New York: Pathfinder.

The Prairie New Democrat Commonwealth. 1966. "Policy Statements and Resolutions: From Saskatchewan CCF Provincial Convention." 26, 45.

Ryerson, Stanley. 1960. *The Founding of Canada: Beginnings to 1815.* Toronto: Progress.

Scofield, Heather. 1999a. "Ottawa to Push Through Nisga'a Deal." *Globe and Mail,* October 22, A4.

_____. 1999b. "Ottawa Prices Native Demands at $200 Billion." *Globe and Mail,* October 26, A3.

Shaw, William. 1979. "'The Hand-Mill Gives you the Feudal Lord': Marx's Technological Determinism." *History and Theory* 18.

Shiva, Vandana. 1988. *Staying Alive: Women, Ecology and Development.* London: Zed.

Socialist Worker. 1997. "500 Years of Racism: Defend Native Rights." January 11. 252.

Spartacist Canada. 1990. "Mulroney, Bourassa Prepare Bloody Massacre: Mohawks Caught in Nationalist Crossfire." Fall. 80.

_____. 1995. "Native Peoples Caught in Nationalist Crossfire." September/ October. 105.

Strauss, Leo. 1989a. "Progress or Return? The Contemporary Crises in Western Civilization." In Leo Strauss, *An Introduction to Political Philosophy.* Detroit: Wayne State University Press.

_____. 1989b. "The Three Waves of Modernity." In Leo Strauss, *An Introduction to Political Philosophy.* Detroit: Wayne State University Press.

Swankey, Ben. 1969. "Canada's Native Peoples." *Communist Viewpoint* 11, 2.

Talbot, Steve. 1981. *Roots of Oppression: The American Indian Question.* New York: International.

Temple, Dominique. 1988. "Economicide." *Interculture* 98, 1.

Tinker, George. 1992. "The Full Circle of Liberation." *Soujourners* 21, 8.

Traverso, Enzo, and Michael Löwy. 1990. "The Marxist Approach to the National Question: A Critique of Nimni's Interpretation." *Science and Society* 54, 2 (Summer).

Women and Revolution. 1993. "Racism, Anti-Abortion, Bigotry: Torture of Native Women in Canada." Spring/Summer. 42.

Wuttunee, W.I.C. 1968. "Not only Indians but All-Canadians Are Losing Their Land." *The Commonwealth* 28, 41.

York, Geoffrey, and Loreen Pindera. 1991. *People of the Pines.* Toronto: Little, Brown.